SO YOU THINK YOU'RE WELL EDUCATED

What Every Well-Educated Person Should Know

RICHARD T. RYAN

QUINLAN PRESS
Boston

Published by Quinlan Press
131 Beverly Street
Boston, MA 02114

Library of Congress
Catalog Card Number 87-63274

ISBN 1-55770-046-X

Printed in the United States of America
May 1988

DEDICATION

This book is dedicated to the memory of
Roger W. Powell III
— gentleman, scholar, and dear friend —

ACKNOWLEDGEMENTS

As an educator, I insist that my students acknowledge their sources when they write; after all, one must give credit where credit is due. The following people have been my sources. They have all helped me with this book in some way, and I am deeply indebted to them for their assistance.

As always, my biggest debt is to my wife, Grace, who keeps me sane even in the craziest of times. I would also like to thank Lou Giletta, Bill Franz, Joe and Diane Sclafani, Virginia Rober, Mike Cassidy, Maryann Milano, Jim and Lois Lamb, Stephen Doglio, and Louis and Mary Ann Wein. Special thanks also go to my daughter, Kaitlin, who is a constant source of inspiration to me.

Finally, I would like to thank my editor, Sandy Bielawa, who makes my job so much easier; and Lorrie Piatczyc and the rest of the staff at Quinlan.

Richard T. Ryan
February 1988

Contents

History

1. Who succeeded Caesar Augustus as emperor of the Roman Empire?
    a) Nero
    b) Claudius
    c) Tiberius
    d) Hadrian

2. Which of the following was the first nation to withdraw from the United Nations?
    a) Indonesia
    b) The Belgian Congo
    c) South Vietnam
    d) Iran

3. What British monarch sat on the throne longer than any other?
    a) Henry VIII
    b) George III
    c) Victoria
    d) King John I

4. Which first lady is sometimes referred to as "the first lady President"?
    a) Mary Todd Lincoln
    b) Julia Dent Grant
    c) Ellen Louise Axxon Wilson
    d) Florence King DeWolf Harding

5. Speaking of the presidency, how many Civil War generals later went on to assume command of the Oval Office?

   a) 3   c) 5
   b) 4   d) 6

6. Which fort was being shelled while Francis Scott Key was composing "The Star Spangled Banner"?

   a) Fort Lowell   c) Fort Wilderness
   b) Fort Sumter   d) Fort McHenry

7. Kettle Hill is better known in American history by what name?

   a) Bunker Hill   c) Pork Chop Hill
   b) San Juan Hill   d) Hamburger Hill

8. Who appointed Adolph Hitler chancellor of Germany in 1933?

   a) Gen. Erich Ludendorff c) Paul von Hindenburg
   b) Dr. Josef Goebbels   d) Hitler, himself

9. Although it may seem something of a contradiction, one American general was awarded the Nobel Peace Prize. Who was he?

   a) Gen. Omar Bradley   c) Gen. Douglas MacArthur
   b) Gen. George Marshall d) Gen. Dwight Eisenhower

10. In what year was the Battle of Waterloo fought?

    a) 1812   c) 1818
    b) 1815   d) 1828

11. Which King of France had the shining sobriquet of "The Sun King" bestowed upon him?

    a) Louis XIII   c) Philip Augustus
    b) Louis XIV   d) Philip the Fair

12. How many federal holidays are there in a single year?

    a) 9   c) 11
    b) 10   d) Not enough

13. Although Lincoln was the first president to lose his life while in office, he was not the first to have an attempt made on his life. Who was?

    a) John Adams   c) Andrew Jackson
    b) Thomas Jefferson   d) Martin Van Buren

14. Franklin was the original name of which of the fifty states?

    a) Tennessee   c) Vermont
    b) Pennsylvania   d) Texas

15. How many men signed the Declaration of Independence?

    a) 13   c) 56
    b) 28   d) 130

16. In that same vein, how many men signed both the Declaration of Independence and the United States Constitution?

    a) None   c) 6
    b) 3   d) 13

17. How many theses did Martin Luther post on the cathedral door in 1517, thus setting the scene for the Protestant Reformation?

    a) 56   c) 159
    b) 95   d) 212

18. Which United States Supreme Court justice served the longest term on the bench?

    a) John Marshall   c) William O. Douglas
    b) Oliver Wendell   d) Byron "Whizzer" White
       Holmes

19. How many bills issued by the United States Treasury are not graced with the portraits of presidents?

    a) None
    b) 2
    c) 3
    d) 5

20. How long did the Hundred Years' War actually last?

    a) 94 years
    b) 108 years
    c) 116 years
    d) 132 years

21. How many U.S. battleships were present at Pearl Harbor on December 7, 1941?

    a) 6
    b) 9
    c) 11
    d) 17

22. What was the name of the act which became the law used to enforce Prohibition?

    a) The Taft-Hartley Act
    b) The Volstead Act
    c) The Mann Act
    d) The Embargo Act

23. In 1215 King John of England was forced to sign the Magna Carta. What is the name of the meadow in which this historic document was ostensibly signed?

    a) Windsor
    b) Hampton Court
    c) Runnymede
    d) Stratford-on-Avon

24. In which year did China conduct its first nuclear bomb test?

    a) 1964
    b) 1966
    c) 1968
    d) 1970

25. Who was the first man to voyage into outer space on two occasions?

    a) Alan Shepard
    b) Gus Grissom
    c) Yuri Gagarin
    d) Gherman S. Titov

26. How many Americans were held hostage by Iran?

    a) 44   c) 52
    b) 48   d) 56

27. In which year was the first hydrogen bomb exploded?

    a) 1949   c) 1958
    b) 1952   d) 1961

28. The Second Triumvirate of the Roman Empire consisted of all of the following except whom?

    a) Augustus Caesar   c) Sextus Pompey
    b) Mark Antony   d) Lepidus

29. Who succeeded Gen. Douglas MacArthur as commander of the U.N. forces?

    a) Gen. Joseph Stillwell   c) Gen. William Westmoreland

    b) Gen. Matthew   d) Gen. George Marshall
       Ridgeway

30. What newspaper achieved a degree of notoriety when it ran the headline "Dewey Defeats Truman"?

    a) *St. Louis Post*   c) *New York Sun*
       Dispatch   d) *Cleveland Plain Dealer*
    b) *Chicago Daily*
       Tribune

31. Which state first gave women the right to vote?

    a) Massachusetts   c) Wyoming
    b) Georgia   d) Oregon

32. Who shot Archduke Francis Ferdinand in 1914 and thus indirectly precipitated World War I?

    a) Gavrilo Princip   c) Edmond Genet
    b) Isfan Mensur   d) Phillippe Grimke

33. How much did the United States pay Napoleon for the Louisiana Purchase?

    a) $5,000,000   c) $18,000,000
    b) $15,000,000   d) $23,000,000

34. Twice in history the United States has had three presidents in a single year. Can you come up with the correct pair of years?

    a) 1841 and 1881   c) 1841 and 1885
    b) 1845 and 1885   d) 1881 and 1900

35. Speaking of the presidency, who was the first president to visit a foreign country while in office?

    a) Polk   c) Teddy Roosevelt
    b) Garfield   d) Wilson

36. Can you name the only family that had a general in both the American Revolution and the Civil War?

    a) Grant   c) Jackson
    b) Sherman   d) Lee

37. On exactly what day of the month does the infamous "Ides of March" fall?

    a) Twelfth   c) Fifteenth
    b) Thirteenth   d) Eighteenth

38. What is inscribed on the tablet held by the Statue of Liberty?

    a) July 4, 1776   c) *E Pluribus Unum*
    b) "In God We Trust"   d) "Give me your tired, your
                               poor, your huddled masses
                               yearning to breathe
                               free . . ."

39. Doroteo Arango was the real name of which of the following?

    a) Gen. Santa Anna   c) Simon Bolivar
    b) Fidel Castro   d) Pancho Villa

40. How many states made up the Confederacy?

    a) 9   c) 11
    b) 10   d) 12

41 What was the name of the ship on which Napoleon surrendered after Waterloo?

    a) *H.M.S. Avenger*   c) *H.M.S. Victory*
    b) *H.M.S. Bellerophon* d) *The Golden Hind*

42. Who was Giuseppe Zangara attempting to assassinate when he shot and killed Chicago mayor Anton J. Cermak?

    a) Woodrow Wilson   c) Gerald Ford
    b) Franklin D. Roosevelt   d) Harry Truman

43. Who succeeded to the British throne in 1660, displacing the commonwealth established by Oliver Cromwell?

    a) James II   c) William of Orange
    b) Charles II   d) George I

44. What was the first women's college in the United States? It was established in 1837.

    a) Vassar   c) Mount Holyoke College
    b) Radcliffe   d) Bryn Mawr

45. Which New York newspaper once employed Karl Marx as a foreign correspondent?

    a) *Daily Mirror*   c) *New York Tribune*
    b) *New York Sun*   d) *Herald Tribune*

46. Which Civil War Battle is also called "the first battle of Manassas"?

    a) Bull Run
    b) Shiloh
    c) Antietem
    d) The Battle of the Wilderness

47. What was the capital of the Confederacy?

    a) Richmond, Virginia
    b) Montgomery, Alabama
    c) Atlanta, Georgia
    d) Charlotte, South Carolina

48. Which is the only one of the fifty states with two official languages?

    a) Hawaii
    b) Louisiana
    c) New Mexico
    d) Delaware

49. What was the name of the Wright Brothers' first plane?

    a) *Kittyhawk*
    b) *Eagle*
    c.) *Discovery*
    d) *Flyer*

50. Traditionally, aircraft carriers are named for battles. What, then, are battleships named for?

    a) Dead war heroes
    b) Cities
    c) States
    d) Presidents

51. What is the oldest city in the United States?

    a) Boston, Massachusetts
    b) San Diego, California
    c) Roanoke, Virginia
    d) St. Augustine, Florida

52. How many of the fifty states have been officially designated as commonwealths?

    a) None
    b) 4
    c) 26
    d) All of them

53. Who was the most frequently elected prime minister of Great Britain?

    a) Churchill   c) Gladstone
    b) Disraeli   d) Chamberlain

54. Which political group sought to ban Catholics and foreigners from public office and to make immigrants live in America for twenty-one years before becoming citizens?

    a) Populist Party   c) Progressive Party
    b) Know Nothing Party   d) Free Soil Party

55. July 16, 1945, is an important date in history for what reason?

    a) The first atomic   c) Mussolini was deposed in
       bomb was exploded   in Italy.
       in New Mexico.   d) Seven years later your
    b) Hitler's generals   author would be born.
       attempted to
       assassinate him.

56. All of the following except whom authored the *Federalist* papers?

    a) Alexander Hamilton   c) John Jay
    b) Thomas Jefferson   d) James Madison

57. Which president established the Environmental Protection Agency?

    a) Kennedy   c) Nixon
    b) Johnson   d) Carter

58. Which president holds the dubious distinction of having filled various government and cabinet posts with members of the "Ohio Gang"?

    a) Taft   c) Grant
    b) Harding   d) Andrew Johnson

59. Who was the first United States president to serve a single term?

    a) John Adams   c) James Monroe
    b) James Madison   d) John Quincy Adams

60. Persons in the North who sympathized with the South during the Civil War were known by which nickname?

    a) Tammany Tigers   c) Copperheads
    b) Mugwumps   d) Dixiecrats

61. Which of the following is generally regarded as "the father of history"?

    a) Heroditus   c) Pliny the Elder
    b) Tacitus   d) Socrates

62. One of the most famous battles in history was the Battle of Hastings, fought in 1066. William the Conqueror was victorious; whom did he defeat?

    a) Earl Godwin   c) Athelred the Unready
    b) Prince Harold   d) King Stephen

63. What was the name of the cartoonist who created the Democratic donkey and the Republican elephant? He also created Santa Claus as we recognize him.

    a) Upton Sinclair   c) Thomas Nast
    b) George Luks   d) Charles Schulz

64. Only one other president besides John F. Kennedy is buried in Arlington National Cemetery. Can you name him?

    a) Andrew Jackson   c) Grover Cleveland
    b) William H. Taft   d) Calvin Coolidge

65. Robert Stroud is perhaps better known as which of the following?

    a) The founder of the American Labor Movement
    b) The inventor of the reaper
    c) Johnny Appleseed
    d) The Bird Man of Alcatraz

66. Which is the only one of the fifty states without an official state nickname?

    a) Alaska
    b) Hawaii
    c) Utah
    d) Idaho

67. As long as we're on the subject of the states, everyone knows that Alaska and Hawaii were the 49th and 50th states. Which was the 48th state?

    a) Oklahoma
    b) Arizona
    c) Nevada
    d) Iowa

68. Which president established the National Collegiate Athletic Association to prevent so many young men from being killed while playing football?

    a) Benjamin Harrison
    b) William McKinley
    c) Theodore Roosevelt
    d) Herbert Hoover

69. Which individual served the shortest term as an elected United States president?

    a) James Buchanan
    b) William Henry Harrison
    c) James Polk
    d) Millard Fillmore

70. At the other end of the spectrum, who was the longest reigning monarch in Europe?

    a) Queen Victoria of England
    b) King Louis XIV of France
    c) King Michael of Greece
    d) King Philip of Spain

71. What state did Senator Joseph McCarthy, who started the communist witch-hunts in the 1950s, represent?

    a) Minnesota
    b) Wisconsin
    c) Indiana
    d) Montana

72. George Custer was the youngest American ever to attain the rank of general. Exactly how old was Custer when he made the grade?

    a) 21
    b) 23
    c) 27
    d) 31

73. Which British monarch had Westminster Abbey built?

    a) William the Conqueror
    b) Edward the Confessor
    c) King Richard the Lion-Hearted
    d) Queen Elizabeth I

74. We have already mentioned Waterloo in several other questions. In what European country is it located?

    a) Holland
    b) Belgium
    c) France
    d) Austria

75. Which king of France was the husband of Marie Antoinette?

    a) Louis XIII
    b) Louis XIV
    c) Louis XV
    d) Louis XVI

76. Which pope in 1303 transferred his court from Rome to Avignon and thus began the "Babylonian Captivity"?

    a) John XII
    b) Leo X
    c) Urban II
    d) Clement V

77. What was the name of Colonel John Glenn's space capsule in which he became the first American to orbit the globe?

    a) Mercury III
    b) Friendship 7
    c) Apollo
    d) Gemini I

78. The first monarch to advance the theory of the Divine Right of Kings was

    a) James I of England   c) Charles I of England
    b) Louis XIV of France   d) Henry VIII of England

79. Which pope is largely credited as the impetus for the First Crusade?

    a) Clement VI   c) Urban II
    b) Julius I   d) Honorius III

80. The earliest code of civil law was devised by King Hammurabi. What empire did he rule?

    a) Assyrian   c) Chaldean
    b) Babylonian   d) Egyptian

81. Which battle is often regarded as the turning point of the Civil War?

    a) Gettysburg   c) Antietem
    b) Vicksburg   d) Second Battle of Bull Run

82. Where did the British general surrender to Washington to end the Revolution?

    a) Saratoga   c) Williamsburg
    b) Yorktown   d) Boston

83. Which war caused the deaths of more American servicemen than any other?

    a) Civil War   c) World War II
    b) World War I   d) Vietnam

84. Which case gave the Supreme Court the right to declare a law unconstitutional?

    a) *Plessy* vs. *Ferguson*   c) *McCulloch* vs. *Maryland*
    b) *Marbury* vs. *Madison*   d) *Brown* vs. *The Topeka
                                      Board of Education*

85. Which war is also known as the "Seven Years' War"?
    a) King George's War   c) War of the Roses
    b) French and Indian   d) Revolutionary War
       War

86. Which of the original thirteen colonies was founded as a Catholic colony?
    a) Virginia   c) Maryland
    b) Georgia   d) New Jersey

87. All except which of the following islands played significant roles in the life of Napoleon?
    a) Corsica   c) St. Helena
    b) Elba   d) Sardinia

88. Which was the first state to secede from the Union in the Civil War?
    a) Georgia   c) North Carolina
    b) Maryland   d) South Carolina

89. How many points did President Woodrow Wilson have in his plans for peace after World War I?
    a) 9   c) 14
    b) 12   d) 21

90. Who is next in line to succeed to the Presidency after the Vice President, Speaker of the House, and President *pro tempore* of the Senate?
    a) Attorney General   c) Senate Majority Leader
    b) Secretary of State   d) House Majority Leader

91. How many permanent members are there in the United Nations Security Council?
    a) 5   c) 9
    b) 7   d) 15

92. Who was the only president to serve as a congressman after he had served as president?

    a) Jefferson   c) John Quincy Adams
    b) Monroe   d) Andrew Johnson

93. Whom did Mao Zedong choose as his successor in the Chinese Communist Party?

    a) Deng Xiaoping   c) Hua Guofeng
    b) Zenko Suzuki   d) Chiang Ching

94. John F. Kennedy was our first Catholic president. Who was the first president without any religious affiliation?

    a) Washington   c) Polk
    b) Jefferson   d) Lincoln

95. Speaking of the Presidency, how many members are there in the electoral college?

    a) 336   c) 538
    b) 432   d) 637

96. What was the name of the first child born in the New World?

    a) Miniver Cheevy   c) Roger Williams
    b) Virginia Dare   d) George Burns

97. What was the name of the American Indian leader who was also known as King Philip?

    a) Pontiac   c) Metacomet
    b) Tecumseh   d) Osceola

98. Who organized the National Women Suffrage Association?

    a) Carrie Nation   c) Dorothea Dix
    b) Susan B. Anthony   d) Bella Abzug

99. Who was the youngest man ever to become President of the United States?

    a) James Monroe   c) Theodore Roosevelt
    b) Franklin Pierce   d) John F. Kennedy

100. Which President had as his presidential administration slogan "The Square Deal"?

    a) Theodore Roosevelt   c) Harry Truman
    b) Franklin Roosevelt   d) Woodrow Wilson

Answers

1.   c) Tiberius

2.   a) Indonesia

3.   c) Queen Victoria ruled from 1837 until 1901.

4.   c) Ellen Louise Axxon Wilson

5.   c) 5

6.   d) Fort McHenry

7.   b) San Juan Hill

8.   c) Paul von Hindenburg, who was president of the German republic

9.   b) Gen. George Marshall was awarded the Nobel Peace Prize in 1953.

10. b) 1815

11. b) Louis XIV

12. b) 10

13. c) Andrew Jackson

14. a) Tennessee

15. c) 56

16. c) 6

17. b) 95

18. c) William O. Douglas served from 1939 until 1975.

19. c) 3: Alexander Hamilton ($10), Benjamin Franklin ($100) and banker Salmon P. Chase ($10,000) — the latter is no longer printed by the U.S. Mint.

20. c) 116 years

21. b) 9

22. b) The Volstead Act

23. c) Runnymede

24. a) 1964

25. b) Virgil "Gus" Grissom

26. c) 52

27. b) 1952

28. c) Sextus Pompey

29. b) Gen. Matthew Ridgeway

30. b) *Chicago Daily Tribune*

31. c) Wyoming

32. a) Gavrilo Princip

33. b) $15,000,000

34. a) 1841 and 1881

35. c) Teddy Roosevelt

36. d) The Lee family

37. c) Fifteenth

38. a) July 4, 1776

39. d) Pancho Villa

40. c) 11

41. b) Napoleon surrendered aboard the *H.M.S. Bellerophon* on July 15, 1815.

42. b) Franklin D. Roosevelt

43. b) Charles II

44. c) Mount Holyoke College

45. c) *New York Tribune*

46. a) Bull Run

47. b) Montgomery, Alabama

48. c) New Mexico—the two languages are English and Spanish.

49. d) Appropriately enough, it was named *Flyer.*

50. c) States

51. d) St. Augustine, Florida, was settled in 1565.

52. b) 4: Kentucky, Massachusetts, Pennsylvania and Virginia.

53. c) Gladstone was elected prime minister on four separate occasions.

54. b) Know Nothing Party

55. a) The first atomic bomb was exploded in New Mexico.

56. b) Thomas Jefferson

57. c) Nixon established the EPA in 1970.

58. b) Harding

59. a) John Adams

60. c) Copperheads

61. a) Heroditus

62. b) Prince Harold

63. c) Thomas Nast, from whose name we get the word "nasty"

64. b) William H. Taft

65. d) The Bird Man of Alcatraz

66. a) Alaska

67. b) Arizona was the last of the forty-eight contiguous states to be admitted to the Union.

68. c) Theodore Roosevelt

69. b) William Henry Harrison's term of office was only thirty-one days.

70. b) Louis XIV of France ruled for seventy-two years.

71. b) Wisconsin

72. b) 23

73. b) Edward the Confessor

74. b) Belgium

75. d) Louis XVI

76. d) Clement V

77. b) Friendship 7

78. a) James I of England

79. c) Urban II

80. b) Babylonian

81. a) Gettysburg

82. b) Yorktown

83. c) World War II

84. b) *Marbury* vs. *Madison*

85. b) French and Indian War

86. c) Maryland

87. d) Sardinia

88. d) South Carolina

89. c) 14

90. b) Secretary of State

91. a) 5

92. c) John Quincy Adams

93. c) Hua Guofeng

94. b) Thomas Jefferson

95. c) 538

96. b) Virginia Dare

97. c) Metacomet

98. b) Susan B. Anthony

99. c) Theodore Roosevelt

100. a) Theodore Roosevelt

Science and Mathematics

1. Which period immediately follows the Paleolithic period?

   a) Neolithic period   c) Bronze Age
   b) Mesolithic period   d) Iron Age

2. Who established the theory that microbes cause disease?

   a) Edward Jenner   c) Jonas Salk
   b) Robert Koch   d) Joseph Lister

3. 852^0 is equal to

   a) 0   c) .852
   b) 1   d) 852

4. "To every force, there is an equal and opposing force" is which of Newton's laws?

   a) First   c) Third
   b) Second   d) Fourth

5. Gregor Mendel is best remembered for his work in which of the following fields?

a) Genetics   c) Cryogenics
b) Cybernetics   d) Radiology

6. $V = 4/3\,\pi\,r^2$ is the formula for the volume of what shape?

a) Pyramid   c) Sphere
b) Cone   d) Cylinder

7. What vitamin is necessary for normal blood clotting?

a) A   c) E
b) B   d) K

8. The normal body temperature is 98.6° Fahrenheit. What is that temperature on the centigrade scale?

a) 32°   c) 68°
b) 37°   d) 112°

9. What is a parallelogram that has four congruent sides?

a) Trapezoid   c) Rhombus
b) Rectangle   d) Kite

10. Approximately how many pints of blood are there in the normal human body?

a) 8   c) 12
b) 10   d) 15

11. At what temperature do the Farenheit and centigrade scales meet?

a) 212°   c) -167°
b) -40°   d) 14°

12. What is a triangle that has no equal sides called?
a) equilateral   c) right
b) isoceles   d) scalene

13. Which planet in Earth's solar system has the greatest number of moons?

    a) Jupiter   c) Uranus
    b) Saturn   d) Neptune

14. Who was the first surgeon to successfully transplant a human heart?

    a) Dr. Christian Barnard c) Dr. Anton Jarvik
    b) Dr. Michael Debakey   d) Dr. Barney B. Clark

15. What is a number called that has only two factors?

    a) Integer   c) Prime number
    b) Composite number d) Rational number

16. Which of the following biological terms is most specific?

    a) Family   c) Order
    b) Genus   d) Species

17. What is the temperature of absolute zero?

    a) -143°C   c) -329°C
    b) -273°C   d) -459°C

18. How long is a rod?

    a) 12 feet   c) 22 feet
    b) 16 feet, 6 inches d) 24 feet, 4 inches

19. To the nearest thousand, what is the speed of light?

    a) 152,000 miles per   c) 186,000 miles per second
       minute   d) 356,000 miles per minute
    b) 174,000 miles per
       second

20. Excluding Earth, what was the first planet to have a man-made object land on it?

    a) Mercury   c) Venus
    b) Mars   d) Saturn

21. How many years equal a millenium?

    a) 1,000   c) 100,000
    b) 10,000   d) 1,000,000

22. How many bones are there in the human body?
    a) 132   c) 417
    b) 206   d) 538

23. What is the effect of Earth's rotation on the wind called?

    a) Geotropism   c) Coriolis force
    b) Aurora borealis   d) Autocatalysis

24. The square root of 125 is between which two numbers?

    a) 11 and 12   c) 12 and 13
    b) 24 and 25   d) 62 and 63

25. Although each snowflake is unique, they all have the same number of sides. How many sides does a snowflake have?

    a) 4   c) 8
    b) 6   d) 12

26. To date, how many elements are there in the Periodic Table?

    a) 4   c) 108
    b) 96   d) 132

27. a + (b + c) = (a + b) + c is an example of which of the following?

    a) Distributive property c) Associative property
    b) Commutative property   d) Identity property

28. The number "1" followed by one hundred zeros is called what?

    a) Centillion   c) Googolplex
    b) Googol   d) The National Debt

29. Which scientist authored the revolutionary tract *Concerning the Revolutions of the Celestial Bodies?*

    a) Ptolemy   c) Kepler
    b) Copernicus   d) Galileo

30. The supplement of a 48-degree angle is an angle of what degree?

    a) 52°   c) 2°
    b) 132°   d) 312°

31. Except for sex cells, how many chromosomes are contained in an ordinary human cell?

    a) 13   c) 26
    b) 23   d) 46

32. What is the blood alcohol level at which a person is declared legally drunk in most states?

    a) .025   c) .1
    b) .05   d) .2

33. Which is a polygon with seven sides?

    a) Hexagon   c) Heptagon
    b) Decagon   d) Quadrilateral

34. What is the chemical symbol for silver?

    a) Ag   c) Fe
    b) Au   d) Si

35. How many calories are there in a single pound?

a) 350   c) 35,000
b) 3,500   d) Who really cares?

36. In a jar containing red and green jelly beans, the ratio of green jelly beans to red jelly beans is 5:3. If the jar contains a total of 160 jelly beans, how many are red?

a) 36   c) 60
b) 45   d) 100

37. How many pairs of nerves branch out from the spinal cord?

a) 22   c) 43
b) 31   d) 96

38. Which of the following scientists is credited with discovering penicillin?

a) Dr. Albert Sabin   c) Alexander Fleming
b) Dr. Jonas Salk   d) Louis Pasteur

39. If a 10-foot flagpole casts a 15-foot shadow, how long will the shadow of a 30-foot flagpole be?

a) 45 feet   c) 180 feet
b) 90 feet   d) 450 feet

40. Which is the largest part of the brain?

a) Cerebrum   c) Cerebellum
b) Medulla   d) Occipital lobe

41. Bacteria reproduce by which method?

a) Budding   c) Miosis
b) Fission   d) Mitosis

42. A coat is selling for $48 after a 20 percent discount. What was the original price of the coat?

a) $54   c) $64
b) $60   d) $72

43. The lion, house cat, leopard and tiger each belong to a different _____.

    a) phylum   c) class
    b) species   d) genus

44. What do we call molten rock that flows from a volcano and turns into solid rock when cool?

    a) Obsidian   c) Scoria
    b) Magma   d) Pumice

45. What number can be written as $8C + 3$ when C is a positive integer?

    a) 13   c) 33
    b) 27   d) 86

46. $C_6 H_{12} O_6$ is the basic chemical formula for which of the following?

    a) carbon   c) sugar
    b) protein   d) hydrogen

47. Earth's crust is made up of 95 percent of which substance?

    a) Igneous rock   c) Sedimentary rock
    b) Metamorphic rock   d) Water

48. Which of the following numbers is closest to 7?

    a) 6.8   c) 7.02
    b) 7.19   d) 6.84

49. Which of the following did Jonas Salk develop?

    a) Smallpox vaccine   c) Measles vaccine
    b) Polio vaccine   d) Rubella

50. What will the result be if you employ the mathematical formula S^3?

a) Volume of a rectangle   c) Volume of a pyramid
b) Volume of a cylinder   d) Volume of a cube

51.   Can you match the technical name for the group on the left with the appropriate animals on the right?

a) Bale	1. Ants
b) Cast	2. Crows
c) Colony	3. Foxes
d) Bevy	4. Geese
e) Gam	5. Hawks
f) Gaggle	6. Leopards
g) Murder	7. Lions
h) Skulk	8. Quail
i) Leap	9. Turtles
j) Pride	10. Whales

Answers

1. b) Mesolithic period

2. b) Robert Koch

3. b) 1

4. c) Third

5. a) Genetics

6. c) Sphere

7. d) K

8. b) 37°

9. c) Rhombus

10. c) 12

11. b) -40°

12. d) scalene

13. a) Jupiter

14. a) Dr. Christian Barnard

15. c) Prime number

16. d) species

17. b) -273°C

18. b) 16 feet, 6 inches

19. c) The actual speed is 186,272 miles per second.

20. b) Mars

21. a) 1,000 years

22. b) 206

23. c) Coriolis force

24. a) 11 and 12

25. b) 6

26. c) 108

27. c) Associative property

28. b) Googol

29. b) Copernicus

30. b) 132°

31. d) 46

32. c) .1

33. c) Heptagon

34. a) Ag

35. b) 3,500

36. c) 60

37. b) 31

38. c) Alexander Fleming

39. a) 45 feet

40. a) Cerebrum

41. b) Fission

42. b) $60

43. b) species

44. b) Magma

45. b) 27

46. c) Sugar

47. a) Igneous rock

48. c) 7.02

49. b) Polio vaccine

50. d) Volume of a cube

51. a) 9 (a bale of turtles)
     b) 5 (a cast of hawks)
     c) 1 (a colony of ants)
     d) 8 (a bevy of quail)
     e) 10 (a gam of whales)
     f) 4 (a gaggle of geese)
     g) 2 (a murder of crows)
     h) 3 (a skulk of foxes)
     i) 6 (a leap of leopards)
     j) 7 (a pride of lions)

Geography

1. In which country is the Taj Mahal located?
   a) Pakistan   c) Iraq
   b) India   d) Burma

2. What nation did Ceylon become after gaining its independence from Great Britain?
   a) Zaire   c) Djiboti
   b) Chad   d) Sri Lanka

3. Assassinated in 1956, Anastasio Somoza had been president of which of the following countries?
   a) Argentina   c) Guatemala
   b) Chile   d) Nicaragua

4. What states are actually separated by the famous Mason-Dixon Line?
   a) Virginia and Maryland   c) Maryland and Delaware
   b) Maryland and Penn-   d) North Carolina and Virginia
   sylvania

5. What is the real name of the mountain in the Himalayas commonly known as K2?

    a) Mt. Kibo   c) Mt. Pisgah
    b) Mt. Godwin-Austin   d) Mt. Vernon

6. What is the only country that flies a non-rectangular flag?

    a) Belize   c) Nepal
    b) Togo   d) Rwanda

7. Can you match up the country on the left with the correct capital on the right?

    a) Afghanistan   1. Asuncion
    b) Bulgaria   2. Budapest
    c) Chile   3. Godthaab
    d) Greenland   4. Kabul
    e) Hungary   5. Monrovia
    f) Liberia   6. Rabat
    g) Morocco   7. Salisbury
    h) New Zealand   8. Santiago
    i) Paraguay   9. Sofia
    j) Rhodesia   10. Wellington

8. The translation of which world capital is "The End of the Elephant's Trunk"?

    a) Delhi   c) Herare
    b) Lusaka   d) Khartoum

9. How many countries make up Central America?

    a) 7   c) 10
    b) 9   d) 12

10. In that same vein, how many countries can be found on the continent of South America?

    a) 11   c) 15
    b) 13   d) 17

11. What is the highest metropolis in the world?

    a) La Paz, Bolivia   c) Buenos Aires, Argentina
    b) Lima, Peru   d) Moscow, Russia

12. What country is also known as Bharat?

    a) Afghanistan   c) Tibet
    b) India   d) Syria

13. Mt. Everest is the highest point in the world. What is the exact elevation of Mt. Everest, located on the Nepal-Tiber border?

    a) 22,746   c) 29,028
    b) 25,689   d) 31,716

14. Rhode Island is the smallest of the United States. Which is the next most diminutive?

    a) Delaware   c) New Hampshire
    b) Maine   d) West Virginia

15. Which of the fifty states bills itself as the "Gem State"?

    a) Idaho   c) California
    b) Wyoming   d) Louisiana

16. How many countries comprise the region commonly called Scandinavia?

    a) 2   c) 6
    b) 4   d) 7

17. The Soviet Union is the world's largest country in terms of square miles. Which is the second largest?

    a) China   c) United States
    b) Canada   d) India

18. In which state would you find the source of the Mississippi River?

    a) North Dakota   c) Wisconsin
    b) Minnesota   d) Michigan

19. Mt Logan is the highest point in which of the following countries?

    a) Canada   c) Ireland
    b) England   d) Scotland

20. Which of the following countries uses the *zloty* as its basic unit of currency?

    a) Rumania   c) Albania
    b) Mexico   d) Poland

21. Bolivia is one of only a few countries with two capitals. La Paz is one; what is the other?

    a) Asuncion   c) Sucre
    b) Paramarimbo   d) Quito

22. How many countries make up the Balkan States?

    a) 4   c) 7
    b) 5   d) 9

23. Which state has the legal right to divide itself up into five smaller states any time it so chooses?

    a) Alaska   c) Hawaii
    b) Texas   d) California

24. The deepest part of the ocean is called the Mariana Trench; approximately how deep is it?

    a) 20,000 feet   c) 36,000 feet
    b) 28,000 feet   d) 39,000 feet

25. Which of the following is the most densely populated country in the world?

    a) Bangladesh   c) Monaco
    b) Japan   d) India

26. The famous Khyber Pass joins Afghanistan to which other country?

    a) Iran   c) U.S.S.R.
    b) Pakistan   d) India

27. How many *major* oceans are there in the world?

    a) 4   c) 6
    b) 5   d) 7

28. Which is the only foreign country to have its capital named after a United States president?

    a) Burma   c) Liberia
    b) Jamaica   d) Mauritania

29. Which is the longest mountain range in the world?

    a) Andes   c) Himalayas
    b) Rockies   d) Appalachians

30. The Islas Malvinas are more commonly known by what name?

    a) Canary Islands   c) Falkland Islands
    b) Virgin Islands   d) Marianas

31. Rounded off to the nearest thousand, what is the circumference of the earth at the equator?

    a) 22,000 miles   c) 28,000 miles
    b) 25,000 miles   d) 31,000 miles

32. Which nation has the longest coastline in the world?

    a) Canada   c) United States
    b) China   d) U.S.S.R.

33. The Lake of the Woods, the northernmost point of the forty-eight contiguous states, can be found in which state?

    a) Washington   c) Minnesota
    b) Michigan   d) Maine

34. How many states have capitals named after presidents?

    a) 3   c) 5
    b) 4   d) 6

35. What is the former name of Ho Chi Minh City?

    a) Da Nang   c) Hue
    b) Hanoi   d) Saigon

36. How many countries comprise the United Kingdom?

    a) 3   c) 5
    b) 4   d) 6

37. Which of the following continents showed the least growth in population from 1980 to 1985?

    a) Asia   c) South America
    b) Africa   d) Europe

38. Angel Falls, the highest waterfall in the world, is found in which of the following countries?

    a) Brazil   c) South Africa
    b) Venezuela   d) United States

39. Excluding Australia, a continent, which is the world's largest island?

a) Greenland   c) Madagascar
b) New Guinea   d) Long Island

40. In which state would you find the geographic center of the United States if you consider all fifty states?

a) South Dakota   c) Kansas
b) North Dakota   d) Montana

41. Which is the highest mountain in the forty-eight contiguous states?

a) King's Peak, Utah   c) Mount Ranier, Washington
b) Mount Whitney,   d) Gannet Peak, Wyoming
   California

42. How many countries presently belong to the United Nations?

a) 119   c) 159
b) 129   d) 179

43. Which is the world's most populous city?

a) Bombay   c) Moscow
b) Mexico City   d) Shanghai

44. Death Valley, the lowest point in the United States, is located in what state?

a) Arizona   c) Nevada
b) California   d) Texas

45. Aptly named Lake Superior is the largest of the Great Lakes. Which is the smallest?

a) Huron   c) Erie
b) Michigan   d) Ontario

46. Which European country is made up of twenty-three cantons?

a) France   c) Switzerland
b) Wales   d) The Netherlands

47. Which is the largest desert in the world, at approximately 3,500,000 square miles?

    a) Chihuahuan   c) Mojave
    b) Gobi   d) Sahara

48. Excluding New York, what is the most densely populated city in the United States?

    a) Chicago   c) Miami
    b) Los Angeles   d) Jersey City, New Jersey

49. What is the capital of Australia?

    a) Sidney   c) Canberra
    b) Melbourne   d) Darwin

50. How many countries can be found on the Iberian peninsula?

    a) 1   c) 3
    b) 2   d) 4

51. Which country contains the southernmost capital on the globe?

    a) Chile   c) New Zealand
    b) South Africa   d) Argentina

52. How many time zones are there in the world?

    a) 12   c) 36
    b) 24   d) 48

53. Exactly how many republics make up the Union of Soviet Socialist Republics?

    a) 11   c) 18
    b) 15   d) 31

54. Which is the most densely populated state in the United States?

    a) Delaware   c) Maryland
    b) Rhode Island   d) New Jersey

Answers

1. b) India

2. d) Sri Lanka

3. d) Nicaragua

4. b) Maryland and Pennsylvania

5. b) Mt. Godwin-Austin

6. c) Nepal

7. a) 4 (Kabul, Afghanistan)
    b) 9 (Sofia, Bulgaria)
    c) 8 (Santiago, Chile)
    d) 3 (Godthaab, Greenland)
    e) 2 (Budapest, Hungary)
    f) 5 (Monrovia, Liberia)

g) 6 (Rabat, Morocco)
h) 10 (Wellington, New Zealand)
i) 1 (Asuncion, Paraguay)
j) 7 (Salisbury, Rhodesia)

8. d) Khartoum

9. a) 7

10. b) 13

11. a) La Paz, Bolivia

12. b) India

13. c) 29,028

14. a) Delaware

15. a) Idaho

16. b) 4: Scandinavia is usually considered to be made up of Norway, Sweden, Denmark and Iceland—Finland is sometimes added, but not always.

17. b) Canada

18. b) Minnesota

19. a) Canada

20. d) Poland

21. c) Sucre

22. b) 5: Albania, Bulgaria, Greece, Romania and Yugoslavia — some might also include European Turkey.

23. b) Texas

24. c) 36,000 feet

25. c) Monaco

26. b) Pakistan

27. a) 4

28. c) The capital of Liberia is Monrovia, after President James Monroe.

29. a) Andes

30. c) Falkland Islands

31. b) 25,000 miles

32. a) Canada

33. c) Minnesota

34. b) 4: Jackson, Mississippi; Jefferson City, Missouri; Lincoln, Nebraska; and Madison, Wisconsin.

35. d) Saigon

36. b) The United Kingdom of Great Britain and Northern Ireland is made up of those two countries, as well as Scotland and Wales.

37. d) Europe

38. b) Venezuela

39. a) Greenland

40. a) If we include all fifty states, the geographic center of the U.S can be found in Butte County, South Dakota, west of Castle Rock.

41. b) Mount Whitney, California

42. c) 159

43. d) Shanghai

44. b) California

45. d) Ontario

46. c) Switzerland

47. d) Sahara

48. d) Jersey City, New Jersey

49. c) Canberra

50. b) 2: Spain and Portugal

51. c) New Zealand

52. b) 24

53. b) 15

54. d) New Jersey

Literature

1. Which of the following authors is the all-time sales leader—second only to the Bible?

   a) Agatha Christie
   b) Sir Arthur Conan Doyle
   c) Stephen King
   d) Barbara Cartland

2. How many plays is Shakespeare commonly credited with composing?

   a) 21
   b) 29
   c) 37
   d) 46

3. Speaking of Shakespeare, what is the actual date of *A Midsummer Night's Dream?*

   a) June 23
   b) June 29
   c) July 1
   d) July 8

4. Which Greek playwright is often referred to as ''the father of tragedy''?

a) Aeschylus   c) Euripides
b) Sophocles   d) Aristophanes

5. Which of the following novels was originally titled *The Last Man in Europe?*

a) *Brave New World*   c) *The Time Machine*
b) *War of the Worlds*   d) *1984*

6. Everyone loves a good musical, and *My Fair Lady* is an excellent one. However, it had its origins in a play. Which of the following stage plays served as the inspiration for *My Fair Lady?*

a) Shaw's *Arms and the Man*   c) Shakespeare's *Love's Labours Lost*
b) Shaw's *Pygmalion*   d) Goldsmith's *She Stoops to Conquer*

7. Abraham Lincoln was assassinated while watching a play at Ford's Theatre. What was the name of that particular dramatic endeavor?

a) *Our American Cousin*   c) *Uncle Tom's Cabin*
b) *The Rivals*   d) *Hamlet*

8. What is the best-selling nonfiction book of all time?

a) Webster's *Dictionary*   c) Spock's *Baby and Child Care*
b) Roget's *Thesaurus*   d) Kennedy's *Profiles in Courage*

9. Who authored the oft-misquoted line, here given correctly, "Music has charms that will soothe a savage breast"?

a) William Congreve   c) William Shakespeare
b) John Dryden   d) John Milton

10. What is the name of the title character in D.H. Lawrence's novel *Lady Chatterley's Lover*?

    a) Mellors   c) Quentin
    b) Bartleby   d) Prescott

11. With which of the following authors should we associate Yoknapatawpha County?

    a) Hemingway   c) Faulkner
    b) Updike   d) O'Neill

12. In James Fenimore Cooper's *The Last of the Mohicans,* what was the name of that "noble savage"?

    a) Bumpo   c) Magua
    b) Uncas   d) Sagamore

13. George Gordon was the real name of which of the following well-known literary figures?

    a) William Blake   c) Lord Byron
    b) William Wordsworth   d) Alfred Lord Tennyson

14. All of the following titles are taken from the works of John Donne except which?

    a) *Death Be Not Proud*   c) *For Whom the Bell Tolls*
    b) *No Man Is An Island* d) *The Sound and the Fury*

15. Which of the following poets is credited with inventing *rhyme royal*?

    a) Chaucer   c) Spenser
    b) Shakespeare   d) e e cummings

16. In the *Divine Comedy* Dante condemned three figures to suffer in the innermost circle of hell. Which of the following was not a member of that infamous group?

    a) Brutus   c) Judas
    b) Cassius   d) Nero

17. Which of the following authors is associated with an amanuensis?

    a) Chaucer   c) Milton
    b) Shakespeare   d) Wordsworth

18. What was the occupation of Finnegan in James Joyce's novel *Finnegans Wake*?

    a) Unemployed   c) Undertaker
    b) Bricklayer   d) Tavernkeeper

19. Which literary form is associated with Charles Lamb and Francis Bacon?

    a) Sonnet   c) Essay
    b) Short story   d) Fable

20. An *iamb* is an unstressed syllable followed by a stressed syllable. What do we call the reverse: a stressed syllable followed by an unstressed syllable?

    a) Anapest   c) Trochee
    b) Spondee   d) Boring

21. What was the common penname shared by the Bronte sisters?

    a) Burns   c) Brand
    b) Bell   d) Brobdignag

22. Who was the captain of the ill-fated *Pequod*?

    a) Captain Queeg   c) Captain Ahab
    b) Captain Bligh   d) Captain Crunch

23. In that naval vein, which author created the character of Horatio Hornblower?

a) C. S. Forester
b) Horace Greeley

c) Thomas Babington
   Macauley
d) Nathaniel Hawthorne

24. Who was Anne Hathaway's famous spouse?

a) William Shakespeare
b) William Wordsworth

c) Eugene O'Neill
d) William Faulkner

25. Who is considered to be "the father of lexicography"?

a) Edmund Spenser
b) Samuel Johnson

c) James Boswell
d) Daniel Webster

26. In *The Taming of the Shrew,* what is the name of Katherina's — the title character's — sister?

a) Ophelia
b) Helena

c) Bianca
d) Portia

27. Tom Canty and Hank Morgan are two creations by which of the following authors?

a) Sherwood Anderson
b) Ernest Hemingway

c) William Faulkner
d) Mark Twain

28. Which literary work is connected with the figure of Scheherazade?

a) *The Panchatantra*
b) *The Arabian Nights*

c) *The Decameron*
d) *The Canterbury Tales*

29. Aside from being the title of a Shakespearean play, *All's Well That Ends Well* was also the original title of which of the following great literary works?

a) *All Quiet on the
   Western Front*
b) *Dr. Zhivago*

c) *Crime and Punishment*
d) *War and Peace*

30. Which of the following dramatists is most closely associated with the term "epic theatre"?

    a) Ibsen
    b) O'Neill
    c) Brecht
    d) Strinderg

31. Traditionally, literary epics are written in how many books?

    a) 3 books or multiples thereof
    b) 5 books or multiples thereof
    c) 7 books or multiples thereof
    d) 12 books or multiples thereof

32. Which famous fictional character lived at 632 Elysian Fields?

    a) Don Vito Corleone
    b) Stanley Kowalski
    c) Willy Loman
    d) Sherlock Holmes

33. What is the real name of the title character in *The Count of Monte Cristo?*

    a) Sidney Carton
    b) Edmund Dantes
    c) Philip Nolan
    d) Errol Flynn

34. Although Winston Churchill is commonly credited with it, he did not originate the phrase "iron curtain." From which great author did the great statesman purloin the phrase?

    a) S. T. Coleridge
    b) G. B. Shaw
    c) James Joyce
    d) T. S. Eliot

35. Which of the following is best classified as a *chanson de geste?*

    a) *Don Quixote*
    b) *Song of Roland*
    c) *Beowulf*
    d) *Coriolanus*

36. Which humanist's best known literary effort is the satiric *Gargantua and Pantagruel?*

    a) Erasmus
    b) Racine
    c) Rabelais
    d) Montaigne

37. All of the following authors would be classified as realists except which?

    a) Balzac   c) Dickens
    b) Ibsen   d) Cervantes

38. Who was the first American to capture the Nobel Prize for Literature?

    a) Theodore Dreiser   c) Eugene O'Neill
    b) Sinclair Lewis   d) Pearl S. Buck

39. All except which of the following held the title of Poet Laureate of England?

    a) Wordsworth   c) Tennyson
    b) Robert Southey d) Matthew Arnold

40. James Baldwin authored all of the following except which novel?

    a) *Go Tell It on the*   c) *Notes of a Native Son*
       Mountain   d) *The Fire Next Time*
    b) *Native Son*

41. Which author's masterpiece is the critically acclaimed "The Wasteland"?

    a) Dylan Thomas   c) T. S. Eliot
    b) Ezra Pound   d) W. B. Yeats

42. Who created the character of Mrs. Malaprop in his play *The Rivals* and thus was responsible for the introduction of the word *malapropism* into the English language?

    a) Richard Steele   c) Oliver Goldsmith
    b) Richard Sheridan   d) Norm Crosby

43. What was the scarlet letter that Hester Prynne wore on her bosom?

a) A for Adultress   c) H for Harlot
b) S for Sinner   d) L for Lust

44. Who is hero of *The Red Badge of Courage?*

    a) Henry Fleming   c) Julian West
    b) Nick Adams   d) Stephen Crane

45. Which poetical priest created a new verse form which became known as "sprung rhythm"? Among his poems are "God's Grandeur" and "Pied Beauty."

    a) Matthew Arnold   c) A. E. Housman
    b) Gerard Manley   d) W. H. Auden
       Hopkins

46. Which of the following authors did not do a variation of the Faust theme?

    a) Marlowe   c) Stephen Vincent Benet
    b) Goethe   d) Shakespeare

47. Who serves as Dante's guide through the Inferno and Purgatory in the *Divine Comedy?*

    a) Vergil   c) Charlemagne
    b) Moses   d) Beatrice

48. The author of *Ben-Hur* was a general in the Civil War. Who is he?

    a) Burnside   c) Wallace
    b) Pickett   d) Hooker

49. According to Malory, which of the following was the Grail Knight?

    a) Sir Gawain   c) Sir Lancelot
    b) Sir Galahad   d) Sir Kay

50. The "Crisis of Faith" occurred in which of these literary periods?

    a) Elizabethan   c) Victorian
    b) Romantic   d) Neo-Classical

51. In Eugene O'Neill's *The Hairy Ape,* the title character was actually named

    a) Slick   c) Lefty
    b) Hickey   d) Yank

52. This author's *Waiting for Godot* is one of the foremost examples of the Theatre of the Absurd. Who is he?

    a) Andre Gide   c) Jorge Luis Borges
    b) Samuel Beckett   d) Luigi Pirandello

53. Where does the major difference between an Italian and an English sonnet lie?

    a) Number of lines   c) Rhyme scheme
    b) Meter   d) Themes treated

54. Which author/artist furnished the illustrations for his *Songs of Innocence* and *Songs of Experience*?

    a) Cowper   c) Coleridge
    b) Blake   d) Edward Young

55. Can you match up the author on the left with his or her pseudonym on the right?

    a) Francois Marie Arouet   1. Richard Bachman
    b) Agatha Christie   2. Boz
    c) Samuel Clemens   3. Lewis Carroll
    d) Charles Dickens   4. George Eliot
    e) Charles Lutwidge Dodgson   5. O. Henry
    f) Mary Ann Evans   6. Diedrich Knickerbocker
    g) Washington Irving   7. Saki

h) Stephen King   8. Mark Twain
i) Hector Hugh Munroe   9. Voltaire
j) William Henry Porter   10. Mary Westmacott

56. Who is the beautiful gypsy in *The Hunchback of Notre Dame*?

a) Eglantine   c) Madeleine
b) Esmeralda   d) Constance

57. Who wields the sword Durendel?

a) Beowulf   c) Don Quixote
b) Roland   d) King Arthur

58. How many circles did Dante envision in Hell when he composed the *Inferno*?

a) 3   c) 9
b) 6   d) 12

59. Rodrigo Diaz is better known by what name?

a) El Cid   c) Zorro
b) Don Quixote   d) Fernando Lamas

60. Which of the following women is associated with Svengali?

a) Brett Ashley   c) Maggie Tulliver
b) Thomasin Yeobright   d) Trilby O'Ferrall

61. How many March girls made up Louisa May Alcott's *Little Women*?

a) 3   c) 5
b) 4   d) 6

62. Who is the sole survivor at the conclusion of *Moby Dick*?

a) Ahab   c) Queequeg
b) Ishamael   d) Starbuck

63. Who was the youngest of King Lear's daughters?

    a) Cordelia   c) Regan
    b) Goneril   d) Juliet

64. Which Roman tragedian was ordered killed by the Emperor Nero?

    a) Plautus   c) Terence
    b) Seneca   d) Suetonius

65. Which of the following poets was known as "the laureate of the Confederacy"?

    a) Henry Timrod   c) Francis Parkman
    b) Sidney Lanier   d) Bret Harte

66. Who wrote both "Paul Revere's Ride" and "The Arsenal at Springfield"?

    a) Longfellow   c) Poe
    b) Whitman   d) Dickinson

67. Which poet is most closely associated with the *dramatic monologue* form?

    a) S. T. Coleridge   c) Ogden Nash
    b) Robert Browning   d) Robert Frost

68. Who is often credited with writing the first modern detective story?

    a) Poe   c) Hawthorne
    b) Conan Doyle   d) Christie

69. Which of the following was not a member of the Harlem Renaissance?

    a) Langston Hughes   c) Countee Cullen
    b) Claude McKay   d) James Baldwin

70. Who is often regarded as "the father of American poetry"?

    a) Washington Irving   c) Thomas Paine
    b) William Cullen Bryant d) Jonathan Edwards

71. "The American Scholar" is often called "our *cultural* declaration of independence." Who was its author?

    a) Ralph Waldo Emerson c) Oliver Wendell Holmes, Sr.
    b) Henry David Thoreau d) Robert Lowell

72. Which was the only book to be the number-one best seller two years in a row?

    a) *Love Story*   c) *The Godfather*
    b) *Jonathan Livingston Seagull* d) *Thy Neighbor's Wife*

73. Which was Stephen King's first novel?

    a) *'Salem's Lot*   c) *The Stand*
    b) *Carrie*   d) *The Dead Zone*

74. Mary Shelley, the wife of the poet, authored which gothic classic?

    a) *Dracula*   c) *Dr. Jekyll and Mr. Hyde*
    b) *Frankenstein*   d) *The Portrait of Dorian Gray*

75. Jonathan Swift and Alexander Pope were both highly regarded masters of what literary form?

    a) Drama   c) Satire
    b) Essay   d) Novel

76. *On the Road* was considered the seminal work for the Beat Generation. Who wrote it?

    a) Alan Ginsburg   c) Laurence Ferlinghetti
    b) Jack Kerouac   d) Richard Nixon

Literature—Questions

77. Which of the following words is not derived from a person's name?
    a) Dunce
    b) Maverick
    c) Boycott
    d) Gossip

78. Which English poet died helping the Greeks in their war against Turkey?
    a) Byron
    b) Shelley
    c) Keats
    d) Sir Walter Scott

79. In how many Shakespearean plays does the rascally Sir John Falstaff appear?
    a) 2
    b) 3
    c) 4
    d) 5

80. What is the setting for F. Scott Fitzgerald's *The Great Gatsby*?
    a) St. Paul, Minnesota
    b) Atlanta, Georgia
    c) Long Island, New York
    d) Paris, France

81. The *Ars Poetica* was written by which Roman author?
    a) Vergil
    b) Juvenal
    c) Ovid
    d) Horace

82. All except which of the following were Cavalier poets?
    a) Herrick
    b) Suckling
    c) Lovelace
    d) Herbert

83. *Everyman* is best classified as what type of play?
    a) Miracle
    b) Morality
    c) Passion
    d) Tragedy

84. Which of the following is generally regarded as the first great poet of free verse?
    a) Longfellow
    b) Whitman
    c) Sandberg
    d) cummings

85. Which of the following was not written by Tennessee Williams?

   a) *A Streetcar Named Desire*
   b) *A Moon for the Misbegotten*
   c) *Cat on a Hot Tin Roof*
   d) *The Glass Menagerie*

86. Daniel Defoe is best known as the author of *Robinson Crusoe*; however, he also wrote which other well-known novel?

   a) *Tom Jones*
   b) *Moll Flanders*
   c) *Vanity Fair*
   d) *Swiss Family Robinson*

87. Which of the following Shakespearean plays is set in Scotland?

   a) *King Lear*
   b) *Macbeth*
   c) *Othello*
   d) *The Merchant of Venice*

88. Socrates was attacked in a play written by whom?

   a) Aristophanes
   b) Aeschylus
   c) Sophocles
   d) Xenophon

89. What are the names of the two vagabonds in Steinbeck's *Of Mice and Men*?

   a) Rich and Ed
   b) Lenny and George
   c) Frank and Curly
   d) Bud and Lou

90. Which famous fictional character was created by Bram Stoker?

   a) Shane
   b) Count Dracula
   c) Tom Swift
   d) Tom Jones

91. William Shakespeare is often referred to as The Bard of Avon. *Bard* is a Celtic word meaning what?

   a) Storyteller
   b) Dramatist
   c) Poet
   d) Entertainer

92. Who was known as the "Belle of Amherst"?

    a) Marianne Moore   c) Christina Rosetti
    b) Emily Dickinson   d) Elizabeth Barrett Browning

93. Which of the following is not a "literary epic"?

    a) *The Iliad*   c) *Richard III*
    b) *The Aneid*   d) *Paradise Lost*

94. How many cantos are there in the *Divine Comedy*?

    a) 3   c) 50
    b) 33   d) 100

95. Who wrote *Who's Afraid of Virginia Woolf*?

    a) Herb Gardner   c) Alice B. Toklas
    b) Edward Albee   d) Virginia Woolf

96. Which great literary work survives in only a single manuscript known as *Cotton Vitellius A XV*?

    a) *The Odyssey*   c) *Beowulf*
    b) *Oedipus Rex*   d) *Paradise Lost*

97. How many Brothers Karamazov were there?

    a) 2   c) 4
    b) 3   d) 5

98. Which of the following poets was romantically linked with Lady Caroline Lamb?

    a) Lord Byron   c) William Shakespeare
    b) Alfred Lord Tennyson   d) John Donne

99. Who wrote the science-fiction novel *Monkey Planet* on which the film *Planet of the Apes* was based?

    a) Edith Wharton   c) H.G. Wells
    b) Pierre Boulle   d) Robert Heinlen

100. Which of Shakespeare's comedies is set in the Forest of Arden?

    a) *Much Ado About Nothing*
    b) *Twelfth Night*
    c) *As You Like It*
    d) *A Midsummer Night's Dream*

101. Marcel Proust's great work *Remembrance of Things Past* derives its title from a phrase in which of the following literary works?

    a) *King Lear*
    b) *Paradise Lost*
    c) *A Christmas Carol*
    d) *Tom Sawyer*

102. Which English author is credited with coining the word *pandemonium*?

    a) Chaucer
    b) Spenser
    c) Milton
    d) Robert Burns

Answers

1. b) Sir Arthur Conan Doyle

2. c) 37

3. a) June 23

4. a) Aeschylus

5. d) *1984*

6. b) Shaw's *Pygmalion*

7. a) *Our American Cousin*

8. c) Spock's *Baby and Child Care*

9. a) William Congreve

10. a) Mellors

11. c) Faulkner

12. b) Uncas

13. c) Lord Byron

14. d) *The Sound and the Fury*

15. a) Chaucer

16. d) Nero

17. c) Milton

18. b) Bricklayer

19. c) Essay

20. c) Trochee

21. b) Bell

22. c) Captain Ahab

23. a) C. S. Forester

24. a) William Shakespeare

25. b) Samuel Johnson

26. c) Bianca

27. d) Mark Twain

28. b) *The Arabian Nights*

29. d) *War and Peace*

30. c) Brecht

31. d) 12 books or multiples thereof

32. b) Stanley Kowalski

33. b) Edmund Dantes

34. b) G. B. Shaw

35. b) *Song of Roland*

36. c) Rabelais

37. d) Cervantes

38. b) Sinclair Lewis

39. d) Matthew Arnold

40. b) *Native Son*

41. c) T. S. Eliot

42. b) Richard Sheridan

43. a) A for Adultress

44. a) Henry Fleming

45. b) Gerard Manley Hopkins

46. d) Shakespeare

47. a) Vergil

48. c) Wallace

49. b) Sir Galahad

50. c) Victorian

51. d) Yank

52. b) Samuel Beckett

53. c) Rhyme scheme

54. b) William Blake

55. a) 9 (Francois Marie Arouet/Voltaire)
     b) 10 (Agatha Christie/Mary Westmacott)
     c) 8 (Samuel Clemens/Mark Twain)
     d) 2 (Charles Dickens/Boz)
     e) 3 (Charles Lutwidge Dodgson/Lewis Carroll)
     f) 4 (Mary Ann Evans/George Eliot)
     g) 6 (Washington Irving/Diedrich Knickerbocker)
     h) 1 (Stephen King/Richard Bachman)
     i) 7 (Hector Hugh Munroe/Saki)
     j) 5 (William Henry Porter/O. Henry)

56. b) Esmeralda

57. b) Roland

58. c) 9

59. a) El Cid

60. d) Trilby O'Ferrall

70

61. b) 4: Meg, Jo, Amy and Beth

62. b) Ishmael

63. a) Cordelia

64. b) Seneca

65. a) Henry Timrod

66. a) Longfellow

67. b) Robert Browning

68. a) Poe

69. d) James Baldwin

70. b) William Cullen Bryant

71. a) Ralph Waldo Emerson

72. b) *Jonathan Livingston Seagull*

73. b) *Carrie*

74. b) *Frankenstein*

75. c) Satirists

76. b) Jack Kerouac

77. d) Gossip

78. a) Byron

79. c) 4

80. c) Long Island, New York

81. c) Ovid

82. d) Herbert

83. b) Morality

84. b) Whitman

85. b) *A Moon for the Misbegotten*

86. b) *Moll Flanders*

87. b) *Macbeth*

88. a) Aristophanes

89. b) Lenny and George

90. b) Count Dracula

91. c) Poet

92. b) Emily Dickinson

93. c) *Richard III*

94. d) 100

95. b) Edward Albee

96. c) *Beowulf*

Literature—Answers

97. c) 4, if you count Smerdyakov, the illegitimate one

98. a) Lord Byron

99. b) Pierre Boulle

100. c) *As You Like It*

101. c) *A Christmas Carol*

102. c) Milton

Art and Music

1. Which museum has the largest art collection in the United States?

   a) Guggenheim Museum

   b) National Gallery

   c) New York City's Metro-politan Museum of Art

   d) Museum of Modern Art in New York

2. In which of the following operas does one tenor sell another tenor a house?

   a) *Madame Butterfly*

   b) *Carmen*

   c) *Tosca*

   d) *Aida*

3. What was the name of the sculptor who created Mount Rushmore?

   a) Winslow Homer

   b) Gotzun Borglum

   c) Giorgio DeChirico

   d) Auguste Rodin

4. What was the name of Lawrence Welk's theme song?

    a) "Tiny Bubbles"

    b) "Bubbles in the Wine"

    c) "I'm Forever Blowing Bubbles"

    d) "And a One and a Two..."

5. What was the name of the artistic school that concentrated on the psychological meanings of the images in their paintings in an effort to represent "the real functioning of the mind"?

    a) Impressionism

    b) Dadaism

    c) Abstractionism

    d) Surrealism

6. Who composed "The Wedding March," as well as the Christmas carol "Hark the Herald Angels Sing"?

    a) Mendelssohn

    b) Bach

    c) Schubert

    d) Listz

7. What was the name of the architect who designed the White House?

    a) Thomas Jefferson

    b) Pierre L'Enfant

    c) James Hoban

    d) Benjamin Latrobe

8. The world's most famous museum is probably the Louvre. Who ordered its construction?

    a) Napoleon

    b) King Henry IV of France

    c) King Louis XIV of France

    d) Robespierre

9. Which composer is commonly referred to as "The March King"?

    a) Scott Joplin

    b) John Philip Sousa

    c) Irving Berlin

    d) Bert Bacharach

10. What was the nickname of King Amenophis IV, Tuten-khame's predecessor as pharoah of Egypt, who revolution-ized Egyptian art?

    a) Akhnaton   c) Asurnasirpal
    b) Ankh   d) Imhotep

11. Noble Sissle and Eubie Blake composed which presidential theme song?

    a) "I Like Ike"   c) "All the Way with JFK"
    b) "I'm Just Wild About d) "Georgia on My Mind"
       Harry"

12. What was the name of the most famous and influential Greek sculptor?

    a) Pheidias   c) Praxiteles
    b) Saldali   d) Myron

13. Which rock group was the first to play at New York's Carnegie Hall?

    a) The Rolling Stones   c) The Beatles
    b) Chicago   d) The Doors

14. Who was the first president of the British Royal Academy?

    a) Sir Joshua Reynolds   c) Thomas Gainsborough
    b) John Zoffang   d) Richard Wilson

15. In a modern orchestra, there are normally how many different sections of instruments?

    a) 3   c) 5
    b) 4   d) 6

16. Who painted " American Gothic"?

    a) Grandma Moses   c) Winslow Homer
    b) Grant Wood   d) Salvador Dali

17. The oboe and the basson are played with which of the following?

    a) A reed
    b) A double reed
    c) A mouthpiece
    d) The fingers

18. Who was the only living artist ever to have his work displayed in the Main Gallery of the Louvre?

    a) Paul Gauguin
    b) Pablo Picasso
    c) Vincent Van Gogh
    d) Andy Warhol

19. Which composer do we associate with *k* or *Koechel* numbers?

    a) Bach
    b) Beethoven
    c) Mozart
    d) Vivaldi

20. The technique Michelangelo used to paint the ceiling of the Sistine Chapel was one he borrowed from which master ?

    a) Giotto di Bondonne
    b) Fillippo Brunelleschi
    c) Raphael
    d) Titian

21. "To Anacreon in Heav'n" provided the tune for which of the following?

    a) "America the Beautiful"
    b) "The Star Spangled Banner"
    c) "God Bless America"
    d) "The Itsy Bitsy Spider"

22. Since we were just speaking of Michelangelo and the Sistine Chapel, it seems only fair to ask which Pope commissioned that backbreaking piece of art?

    a) Sixtus IV
    b) Julius II
    c) Urban III
    d) Honorius III

23. Which of Beethoven's symphonies, named the *Eroica*, is

dedicated to Napoleon?

a) #1   c) #5
b) #3   d) #9

24. Which of the following would not be considered a Baroque artist?

a) Rubens   c) Berini
b) Rembrandt   d) Van Eyck

25. To which composer are we indebted for the lovely "Blue Danube"?

a) Listz   c) Handel
b) Schubert   d) Strauss

26. Who designed the Guggenheim Museum on Manhattan's East Side?

a) David Smith   c) Thomas Eakins
b) Frank Lloyd Wright   d) Benjamin Latrobe

27. *Fidelio* is the title of the only opera ever written by this composer. It was originally entitled *Leonore*. Who is the artist in question?

a) Brahms   c) Beethoven
b) Bach   d) Handel

28. Which of the following schools of art had its origins in America?

a) Surrealism   c) Expressionism
b) Abstractionism   d) Abstract Expressionism

29. Can you name the musician who is considered by many to be "the father of the blues"?

a) Scott Joplin   c) Louis Armstrong
b) W. C. Handy   d) Leadbelly

30. Who designed and built the Taj Mahal?

    a) Shah Jehau
    b) Jehrewahl
    c) Nehru
    d) Ghandi

31. What is the title of the well-known Gilbert and Sullivan operetta that is subtitled *The Lass That Loved a Sailor*?

    a) *H.M.S. Pinafore*
    b) *The Pirates of Penzance*
    c) *The Mikado*
    d) *Ruddigore*

32. Which artist is generally regarded as the most important exponent of pure abstraction in the twentieth century?

    a) Andre Derain
    b) Jean Arp
    c) Piet Mondrian
    d) Marc Chagall

33. Bach composed in all of the following forms except which?

    a) Cantata
    b) Oratorio
    c) Opera
    d) Suite

34. Which artist is generally regarded as the founder of Cubism because of his revolutionary work *Les Demoiselles d'Avignon*?

    a) Juan Gris
    b) Pablo Picasso
    c) Salvador Dali
    d) Georges Rouault

35. Who wrote the words to "Hail to the Chief"?

    a) Edgar Allen Poe
    b) Sir Walter Scott
    c) Robert Burns
    d) Charles Dickens

36. Which artist has been dubbed "The Master of Aix"?

    a) Paul Cezanne
    b) Piet Mondrian
    c) Wassily Kandinsky
    d) Raoul Dufy

37. We've all heard it, but do you know who composed *The William Tell Overture*?

    a) Verdi
    b) Rossini
    c) Donazetti
    d) The Lone Ranger

38. "A painting before it is anything else is a flat surface with lines and colors arranged in a certain order" became the central doctrine of modern art. Who set down this dictum?

    a) Georges Seurat
    b) Claude Monet
    c) Maurice Denis
    d) Henri Matisse

39. The first million-selling record was Enrico Caruso's version of the aria *Vesti la giubba*. From which opera does that aria come?

    a) *Pagliacchi*
    b) *The Barber of Seville*
    c) *La Boheme*
    d) *Aida*

40. Which of the following artists is generally regarded as the leader of the group that was known as *Les Fauves*?

    a) Henri Matisse
    b) Maurice Vlaminck
    c) Andre Derain
    d) Georges Seurat

41. Which of the following is generally regarded as the first opera?

    a) *Orfeo*
    b) *II Barbiere di Siviglia*
    c) *Giulio Cesare*
    d) *La Nozze*

42. The term "Impressionism" was derived from a painting entitled *Impression: Sunrise*—by whom?

    a) Cezanne
    b) Monet
    c) Van Gogh
    d) Manet

43. In addition to its famous weekly charts, *Billboard Magazine* also keeps yearly records. According to *Billboard*, which of

the following groups never had a number-one selling album for a given year?

a) The Byrds

b) The Monkees

c) War

d) Fleetwood Mac

44. Christopher Wren is best known for his design of what building?

a) Big Ben

b) St. Paul's Cathedral

c) Westminster Abbey

d) Buckingham Palace

45. Who was presented with the first gold record?

a) Glen Miller

b) Mitch Miller

c) Jimmy Dorsey

d) Enrico Caruso

46. Which architect's *Bauhaus* became the model for what has become known as the "international style" of architecture?

a) F. L. Wright

b) Walter Gropius

c) Mies van der Rohe

d) Le Corbusier

47. Normally, there are how many movements in a symphony?

a) 3

b) 4

c) 5

d) 6

48. One of the most important discoveries in the history of art was the use of foreshortening. Which ancient civilization is generally credited with this artistic revolution?

a) Assyrians

b) Egyptians

c) Greeks

d) Romans

49. Which is the lowest female singing voice?

a) Soprano

b) Mezzo-soprano

c) Contralto

d) Bette Midler's

50. Who was the court painter of King Henry VIII of England?

    a) Jan van Eyck   c) Pieter Brueghel
    b) Hans Holbein   d) Rubens

51. The sculptor who designed the Statue of Liberty modeled the face after his mother's. What was his name?

    a) Bartholdi   c) Rodin
    b) Eiffel   d) L'Enfant

52. Earlier we asked about " The Wedding March"; now we'd like to know who composed the music for "The Bridal March," which is more commonly known as "Here Comes the Bride?"

    a) Mendelssohn   c) Schopin
    b) Wagner   d) Strauss

53. Recently, a painting was sold for a record $53.9 million. What was the name of that costly canvas?

    a) *Sunflowers*   c) *Daffodils*
    b) *Irises*   d) *Roses*

54. What is the more popular name of the painting whose formal title begins "Arrangement in Gray and Black"?

    a) *Whistler's Mother*   c) *Starry Night*
    b) *The Night Watch*   d) *The Blue Boy*

Answers

1. c) New York City's Metropolitan Museum of Art

2. a) *Madame Butterfly*

3. b) Gotzun Borglum

4. b) "Bubbles in the Wine"

5. d) Surrealism

6. a) Mendelssohn

7. c) James Hoban

8. b) King Henry IV of France

9. b) John Philip Sousa

10. a) Akhnaton

11. b) "I'm Just Wild About Harry"

12. a) Pheidias

13. b) Chicago

14. a) Sir Joshua Reynolds

15. b) 4

16. b) Grant Wood

17. b) A double reed

18. b) Pablo Picasso

19. c) Mozart

20. a) Giotto di Bondonne

21. b) "The Star Spangled Banner"

22. b) Pope Julius II

23. b) #3

24. d) Van Eyck

25. d) Strauss

26. b) Frank Lloyd Wright

27. c) Beethoven

28. d) Abstract Expressionism

29. b) W. C. Handy

30. a) Shah Jehau

31. a) *H.M.S. Pinafore*

32. c) Piet Mondrian

33. c) Opera

34. b) Pablo Picasso

35. b) Sir Walter Scott (see *The Lady of the Lake*, Canto II)

36. a) Paul Cezanne

37. b) Rossini

38. c) Maurice Denis

39. a) *Pagliacci*

40. a) Henri Matisse

41. a) *Orfeo*, by Claudio Monteverde

42. b) Monet

43. a) The Byrds

44. b) St. Paul's Cathedral

45. a) Glen Miller

46. b) Walter Gropius

47. b) 4

48. c) Greeks

49. c) Contralto

50. b) Hans Holbein

51. a) Bartholdi

52. b) Richard Wagner

53. b) *Irises*

54. a) *Arrangement in Gray and Black — The Artist's Mother* is more commonly known as "Whistler's Mother."

Philosophy and Theology

1. Which great medieval theologian-philosopher wrote the *Summa Theologica*?
   a) Albertus Magnus c) St. Thomas More
   b) St. Thomas Aquinas d) Abelard

2. Which of the following philosophers did not win a Nobel Prize in Literature?
   a) Sartre c) Bertrand Russell
   b) Camus d) Dostoevsky

3. Who was the first Catholic saint born in America?
   a) John Cardinal c) Elizabeth Bayley Seton
   Neuman d) Father Jacques Marquette
   b) Bishop John Carroll

4. Americans Henry David Thoreau and Ralph Waldo Emerson were proponents of a philosophy known as what?
   a) Idealism c) Rationalism
   b) Logical Positivism d) Transcendentalism

5. What does the word *kosher* in the Jewish religion mean?

    a) Sacred   c) Clean
    b) Holy   d) Proper

6. Which Greek philosopher is credited with establishing the Lyceum school outside of Athens?

    a) Socrates   c) Aristotle
    b) Plato   d) Zeno

7. All of the following are considered "deadly sins" except for which?

    a) Lust   c) Ambition
    b) Sloth   d) Pride

8. Which of the ancient Greeks is often hailed as "the father of cynicism"?

    a) Heroditus   c) Pericles
    b) Diogenes   d) Ptolomey

9. Siddhartha, the founder of Buddhism, had a last name. Which was it?

    a) Mahabharanta c) Singh
    b) Gautama   d) Kaaba

10. Which Greek philosopher was condemned to death for corrupting the young people of Athens?

    a) Socrates   c) Aristotle
    b) Plato   d) Seneca

11. Which of the following religions has not evolved—either directly or indirectly—from Judaism?

    a) Roman Catholicism c) Lutheranism
    b) Islam   d) Shintoism

12. Which philosopher once observed, "Man was born free, and everywhere he is in chains"?

    a) Karl Marx   c) John Stuart Mill
    b) Jean Jacques   d) Blaise Pascal
       Rousseau

13. Which of the Evangelists also authored "The Book of Revelations"?

    a) Matthew   c) Luke
    b) Mark   d) John

14. What is the name of the philosophy that is commonly associated with Kierkegaard, Sartre and Camus, among others?

    a) Absurdism   c) Behaviorism
    b) Existentialism   d) Dialectical Marxism

15. According to the Roman Catholic religion, who is the patron saint of accountants and bookkeepers?

    a) Matthew   c) Luke
    b) Mark   d) John

16. In which of Plato's dialogues do we find a discussion of the "lost city" of Atlantis?

    a) *Phaedo*   c) *Apology*
    b) *Timaeus*   d) *Phaedrus*

17. Which of the following religions has the greatest number of believers?

    a) Buddhism   c) Islam
    b) Hinduism   d) Roman Catholicism

18. Which philosopher is credited with coining the term *dialectic*?

    a) Spinoza   c) Kant
    b) Liebniz   d) Hegel

19. Which is the oldest of the religions listed below?

    a) Buddhism c) Judaism
    b) Confucianism d) Sikhism

20. With which of the following philosophers do we associate the phrase, *Cogito ergo sum*?

    a) Socrates c) Rene Descartes
    b) Thomas Aquinas d) Immanuel Kant

21. The Cisctercians of Strict Observance are better known by what name?

    a) Benedictines c) Trappists
    b) Maryknolls d) Franciscans

22. Who is often regarded as "the first philosopher"?

    a) Hesiod c) Pyrro of Ellis
    b) Thales of Miletus d) King Hammarubi

23. What is the pilgrimage called that Muslims are required to make to Mecca?

    a) *Hegira* c) *Ramadan*
    b) *Hajj* d) *Akimsa*

24. Which branch of philosophy deals with the study of knowledge?

    a) Phenomenalism c) Ontology
    b) Epistomology d) Axiology

25. The *Bhagavad-Gita* is the sacred text for which of the following religions?

    a) Buddhism c) Taoism
    b) Hinduism d) Zoroastrianism

26. Which philosopher invented the term *monads* to describe what he called "thought beings"?

    a) Spinoza   c) Leibniz
    b) Hume   d) Nietzsche

27. Although John Calvin spent most of his life in Switzerland, he was by birth which nationality?

    a) English   c) French
    b) Scottish   d) Dutch

28. Who wrote *The Consolation of Philosophy*?

    a) St. Augustine of   c) Boethius
        Hippo   d) Heraclitus
    b) Duns Scotus

29. Who founded the Jesuit order?

    a) St. Benedict   c) St. Ignatius
    b) St. Francis   d) St. Boniface

30. Which great medieval philosopher-theologian wrote the influential work *Sic et Non*, which is sometimes translated as *Yes and No*?

    a) Albertus Magnus   c) St. Bernard of Clairvaux
    b) Abelard   d) St. Gregory the Great

31. From what mountain did Moses see all of the Promised Land just before he died?

    a) Mount Sinai   c) Mount Ararat
    b) Mount Nebo   d) Mount Rushmore

32. The *Critique of Pure Reason* was the work of which of the following thinkers?

    a) Kant   c) Hegel
    b) Hume   d) Burke

33. Who was the first Christian emperor of the Roman Empire?

    a) Claudius   c) Charlemagne
    b) Constantine   d) Marcus Aurelius

34. Which of the following is not one of Aristotle's "three unities"?

    a) Action   c) Time
    b) Character   d) Place

35. Approximately, how many popes have served as head of the Catholic Church?

    a) 153   c) 264
    b) 201   d) 324

36. Which philosopher was the first to draw up and deal with the idea of a "social contract"?

    a) Locke   c) Rousseau
    b) Hobbes   d) Bacon

37. What date is the beginning of the astrological year?

    a) March 21   c) September 16
    b) June 22   d) January 26

38. In *The Prince* Machiavelli said that a successful ruler must possess the qualities of which two animals?

    a) Wolf and sheep   c) Lion and fox
    b) Bear and eagle   d) Shark and leopard

39. Which of the Evangelists wrote the shortest verse in the Bible: "Jesus wept"?

    a) Matthew   c) Luke
    b) Mark   d) John

40. This philosopher wrote *Beyond Good and Evil* and was one of the first to advance the theory of the "superman." Who was he?

    a) Nietzsche   c) Sartre
    b) Kierkegaard   d) Tillich

41. According to experts in the field, what is the highest order of angel?

    a) Archangels   c) Principalities
    b) Dominations   d) Seraphims

42. Which of the following schools of thought emphasized virtue over pleasure?

    a) Stoicism   c) Zoroastrianism
    b) Epicureanism   d) Manicheism

43. And since turnabout is fair play, what is the school of philosophy that emphasizes pleasure as the highest good?

    a) Neo-Platonism   c) Metaphysics
    b) Hedonism   d) Conventionalism

44. How many books are there in both the Old and New Testaments in the King James Bible?

    a) 39   c) 66
    b) 48   d) 81

45. Which of the following might be called the seminal work of Communism?

    a) *Mein Kampf*   c) *The Origin of Species*
    b) *Das Kapital*   d) *Thus Spake Zarathustra*

46. Who were Shadrach, Meshach and Abednego?

    a) The three men   c) The three sons of Noah
       thrown into the fiery   d) An Old Testament comedy

furnace   team
b) The three wise men

47. A philosopher claiming to be an empiricist emphasizes which of the following?

    a) God
    b) Experience
    c) Reason
    d) Will

48. According to the Bible, who lived to be 969 years old?

    a) Adam
    b) Moses
    c) Methuselah
    d) Abraham

49. Three deities make up the Hindu trinity. They are Brahma, the Creator; Shiva, the Destroyer and Restorer; and Vishnu, who is what?

    a) The God of the Dead
    b) The Savior
    c) The Judge
    d) The God of Nature

50. The Moslem calendar began on September 13, 622. What happened on this date?

    a) God first spoke to Mohammed.
    b) Mohammed fled from Mecca to Medina.
    c) Mohammed was born.
    d) Mohammed died.

Answers

1. b) St. Thomas Aquinas

2. d) Dostoevsky

3. c) Elizabeth Bayley Seton

4. d) Transcendentalism

5. d) Proper

6. c) Aristotle

7. c) ambition

8. b) Diogenes

9. b) Gautama

10. a) Socrates

11. d) Shintoism

12. b) Jean Jacques Rousseau

13. d) John

14. b) Existentialism

15. a) Matthew

16. b) *Timaeus*

17. c) Islam

18. d) Hegel

19. c) Judaism

20. c) Rene Descartes

21. c) Trappists

22. b) Thales of Miletus

23. b) *Hajj*

24. b) Epistomology

25. b) Hinduism

26. c) Leibniz

27. c) French

28. c) Boethius

29. c) St. Ignatius

30. b) Abelard

31. b) Mount Nebo, also called Mount Pisgah

32. a) Kant

33. b) Constantine

34. b) Character

35. c) 264

36. b) Hobbes

37. a) March 21

38. c) Lion and fox

39. d) John

40. a) Nietzsche

41. d) Seraphims

42. a) Stoicism

43. b) Hedonism

44. c) 66

45. b) *Das Kapital*

46. a) The three men thrown into the fiery furnace

47. b) experience

48. c) Methuselah

49. b) The Savior

50. b) Mohammed fled from Mecca to Medina

Mythology

1. Most of our knowledge of Greek mythology is based on the work of whom?

    a) Herodotus
    b) Cincinnatus
    c) Solon
    d) Hesiod

2. In Greek mythology, who was the father of the god Zeus?

    a) Uranus
    b) Cronus
    c) Hestia
    d) Ra

3. What is the only day of the week named for a Roman god?

    a) Tuesday
    b) Thursday
    c) Saturday
    d) Sunday

4. What is the name of the three-headed dog that guards the entrance of Hades?

    a) Pegasus
    b) Minotaur
    c) Cerebus
    d) Pirithous

5. According to legend, how many labors was Hercules required to perform?

   a) 10   c) 13
   b) 12   d) 15

6. Which of the following was the Egyptian god of death?

   a) Horus   c) Oro
   b) Anubis   d) Aton

7. Which of the following was a child of Oedipus?

   a) Iphigenia   c) Creon
   b) Ismene   d) Rex

8. As long as we're on the subject of children, what was the name of Ulysses' son?

   a) Caenis   c) Orestes
   b) Ascanius   d) Telemachus

9. The owl was the symbol of which Greek goddess?

   a) Athena   c) Hera
   b) Aphrodite   d) Iris

10. How many muses were there in Greek mythology?

    a) 3   c) 9
    b) 6   d) 12

11. Although she is always referred to as Helen of Troy, Helen was actually queen of what city?

    a) Athens   c) Thebes
    b) Sparta   d) Ithaca

12. What was the name of the great Roman feast which was a sort of precursor to Christmas?

    a) Bacchanalia c) Robigalia
    b) Saturnalia   d) Mardi Gras

13. Who was the ferryman on the river Styx who brought the souls of the dead to the underworld?

    a) Augeas   c) Dis
    b) Charon   d) Janus

14. In Norse mythology, what types of birds are special to the god Odin?

    a) Owls   c) Hawks
    b) Ravens   d) Eagles

15. Everyone knows that the only place Achilles could be wounded was in the heel. What river was he dipped in as an infant that gave him his near invulnerability?

    a) Cocytus   c) Styx
    b) Acheron   d) Lethe

16. The mythological founders of Rome, Romulus and Remus, were ostensibly raised by what creature?

    a) Eagle   c) Wolf
    b) Lion   d) Bear

17. Who was the son of Tantalus whose left shoulder blade, according to myth, was accidentally eaten by the goddess Demeter?

    a) Atreus   c) Thyestes
    b) Pelops   d) Telamon

18. What is the name of the Cyclops outwitted by Ulysses in *The Odyssey*?

    a) Chiron   c) Charybidis
    b) Scylla   d) Polyphemus

19. In *The Odyssey* Ulysses also encountered a sorceress who

turned men into swine. What was that cunning charmer's name?

a) Calypso   c) Medea
b) Circe   d) Atalanta

20. This god possessed the ability to change shapes at will. By what moniker was this metamorphic immortal known?

a) Poseidon   c) Proteus
b) Vulcan   d) Thor

21. Who was the Queen of the Amazons?

a) Hera   c) Diana
b) Hippolyta   d) Artemis

22. In Greek mythology Menelaus was the husband of Helen and the brother of the Greek commander during the Trojan War. What was that soldier's name?

a) Achilles   c) Ajax
b) Agamemnon   d) Odysseus

23. The Roman goddess Minerva was the counterpart of which Greek goddess?

a) Hestia   c) Athena
b) Hera   d) Artemis

24. In that same vein, the Greek god Hermes became what Roman god?

a) Mars   c) Neptune
b) Mercury   d) Vulcan

25. What was the name of the unfortunate nymph who fell in love with the self-centered Narcissus?

a) Pan   c) Pandora
b) Echo   d) Silvanus

26. According to legend, the Minotaur was the child of a bull and which queen?

   a) Jocasta
   b) Demeter
   c) Androgeus
   d) Paisiphae

27. Who was Daedalus' son, who had the misfortune to fly too close to the sun?

   a) Pegasus
   b) Bellerophon
   c) Icarus
   d) Phaeton

28. Which character is hailed for slaying the Gorgon, Medusa?

   a) Theseus
   b) Hercules
   c) Perseus
   d) Diomedes

29. Who was the young girl who kept prophesying the destruction of Troy but who was ignored because of a curse?

   a) Cassopeis
   b) Cassandra
   c) Hecuba
   d) Electra

30. What is the name of the winged stallion who has flown into prominence as the Mobil logo?

   a) Mercury
   b) Pegasus
   c) Stynphalus
   d) Mobilus

31. Everyone knows a great deal about Hercules, but did you know that the hero also had a half-brother who was born as his twin? What is this oft-overlooked sibling's name?

   a) Iphicles
   b) Autolycus
   c) Cephalus
   d) Cybele

32. Speaking of Hercules' family, what was the name of that immortal's mother?

   a) Alcmene
   b) Penelope
   c) Dido
   d) Creusa

33. Who is blind prophet who figures so prominently in the legend of Oedipus?

    a) Creon
    b) Haemon
    c) Tiresias
    d) Orestes

34. Who is the mother of the god of love, Cupid?

    a) Iris
    b) Juno
    c) Ra
    d) Venus

35. According to the Greeks, the gods made their home on which mountain top?

    a) Ambrosia
    b) Olympus
    c) The Parthenon
    d) The Acropolis

36. At the other end of creation, the Greek god Hades comes to be known in Roman mythology by what name?

    a) Satan
    b) Pluto
    c) Neptune
    d) Poseidon

37. Name the father who may have so infatuated Electra that Freud found her irresistable.

    a) Ulysses
    b) Menelaus
    c) Agamemnon
    d) Ajax

38. According to legend, the city of Troy was also known by what name?

    a) Sparta
    b) Ilium
    c) Minos
    d) Carthage

39. Which of the following did the Romans worship as their god of war?

    a) Jupiter
    b) Mars
    c) Apollo
    d) Ares

40. Which real-life figure is credited with undoing the mythical Gordian Knot?

    a) Julius Caesar   c) Philip of Macedonia
    b) Augustus Caesar   d) Alexander the Great

41. Cuchulain is one of the mythological figures of which of the following countries?

    a) Finland   c) Ireland
    b) Portugal   d) Wales

42. Who is the god of mischief and evil in Norse mythology?

    a) Baldur   c) Hodur
    b) Loki   d) Thor

43. The Egyptians believed in a supreme deity which they identified with the sun. Name this god.

    a) Anubis   c) Isis
    b) Osiris   d) Ra

44. According to Greek mythology, what was the name of the first woman?

    a) Ariadne   c) Pandora
    b) Psyche   d) Persephone

45. *The Mabinogion* is a collection of four tales dealing with the mythological figures of which country?

    a) Spain   c) Wales
    b) Sweden   d) Switzerland

46. According to legend, Paul Bunyan owned a great blue ox. What was her name?

    a) Babe   c) Pumper
    b) Ox   d) Snooze

47. John Chapman became known in American folklore by what name?

    a) John Henry, the steel driving man
    b) Johnny Appleseed
    c) John Brown
    d) Pecos Bill

48. Tuesday is named for a god of which of the following mythologies?

    a) Greek
    b) Roman
    c) Celtic
    d) Norse

49. The tree-worshipping priests of ancient Ireland were known by what name?

    a) Pantheists
    b) Druids
    c) Banshees
    d) Leprechauns

50. According to Greek mythology, how many rivers are there in Hades?

    a) 3
    b) 4
    c) 5
    d) 6

51. In structure, the best word that describes Greek and Roman mythology is _____.

    a) monotheistic
    b) anthropomorphic
    c) heliocentric
    d) teleological

52. In *The Iliad*, who was Achilles' best friend?

    a) Paris
    b) Ajax
    c) Patroclus
    d) Andomoche

53. During the Trojan War, who, according to legend, was the ruler of Troy?

    a) Cyrus
    b) Solon
    c) Thucydides
    d) Priam

Answers

1. d) Hesiod

2. b) Cronus

3. c) Saturday

4. c) Cerebus

5. b) 12

6. b) Anubis

7. b) Ismene

8. d) Telemachus

9. a) Athena

10. c) 9

11. b) Sparta

12. b) Saturnalia

13. b) Charon

14. b) Ravens

15. c) Styx

16. c) Wolf

17. b) Pelops

18. d) Polyphemus

19. b) Circe

20. c) Proteus

21. b) Hippolyta

22. b) Agamemnon

23. c) Athena

24. b) Mercury

25. b) Echo

26. d) Paisiphae

27. c) Icarus

28. c) Perseus

29. b) Cassandra

30. b) Pegasus

31. a) Iphicles

32. a) Alcmene

33. c) Tiresias

34. d) Venus

35. b) Olympus

36. b) Pluto

37. c) Agamemnon

38. c) Ilium

39. b) Mars

40. d) Alexander the Great

41. c) Ireland

42. b) Loki

43. d) Ra

44. c) Pandora

45. c) Wales

46. a) Babe

47.   b) Johnny Appleseed

48.   d) The name "Tuesday" comes from the Norge god of war, Tiw, which is also spelled Twr.

49.   b) Druids

50.   c) 5: Acheron, Cocytus, Phlegethon, Styx and Lethe.

51.   b) Anthropomorphic

52.   c) Patroclus

53.   d) Priam

Visual Aids

1. To which god or goddess was the Parthenon in ancient Greece dedicated?

   a) Zeus

   b) Hera

   c) Athena

   d) Apollo

Photo courtesy the *Staten Island Register*

2. The military man pictured above is best remembered for his famous observation that "Old generals never die; they just fade away." Who is he?

   a) Gen. Omar Bradley   c) Gen. George Marshall

   b) Gen. George Patton   d) Gen. Douglas MacArthur

3. In which state did Abraham Lincoln deliver his famous Gettysburg Address?

   a) Virginia   c) Pennsylvania
   b) Maryland   d) Delaware

4. What is the real name of the Rembrandt painting which has become the symbol for Dutch Masters Cigars?

   a) *The Guild Masters of*   c) *The Burghers of Brussells*
      Amsterdam
   b) *The Syndics of the*   d) *The Town Fathers in*
      Cloth Hall   *Conference*

Photo courtesy the *Staten Island Register*

5. Eugene O'Neill, pictured above, wrote all of the following except

a) *Anna Christie*   c) *Strange Interlude*
b) *The Emperor Jones*   d) *All My Sons*

Portrait by Gilbert Sullivan, now at the National Gallery of Art

6. George Washington led the American forces during the Revolutionary War. What was the name of the British general who finally surrendered to Washington at Yorktown?

a) Burgoyne   c) Cornwallis
b) Clinton   d) Howe

Photo courtesy the *Staten Island Register*

7. Everyone has seen the historic headline "Dewey Defeats Truman," and everyone knows that Truman actually won that election. Who was Truman's vice president who shared in that historic victory?

    a) Henry Agard Wallace   c) Garret A. Hobart
    b) Alban W. Barkley   d) Levi P. Morton

Photo courtesy the *Staten Island Register*

8. At this writing, Nancy Reagan is the First Lady of the United States. What is the first name, spelled correctly, of Mikhail Gorbachev's wife?

    a) Raza   c) Raysah
    b) Raisa   d) Semya

9. What is the real name of the painting above which is commonly known as the *Mona Lisa?*

   a) *La Enigmatica*   c) *La Provacateur*
   b) *La Gioconda*   d) *La Mer*

Photo courtesy the *Staten Island Register*

10. Pictured above is the man who served as the special Watergate prosecutor. What is his name?

    a) Sam Ervin   c) John Sirica
    b) Archibald Cox   d) Robert Bork

Photo courtesy the *Staten Island Register*

11. At this writing, Joan Rivers is the midst of a libel suit claiming that a magazine story run about her "is a total pack of evil, vicious, sick lies." Which magazine is the comedienne suing for $50 million?

   a) *Playboy*   c) *Gentlemen's Quarterly*
   b) *Penthouse*   d) *Mad Magazine*

Photo courtesy the *Staten Island Register*

12. The man above has been called America's leading consumer advocate. He began his career by writing *Unsafe at Any Speed*, an exposé of the auto industry. What is his name?

   a) David Horowitz   c) Bernard Meltzer
   b) Vance Packard   d) Ralph Nader

Photo courtesy the *Staten Island Register*

13. What is Oliver North's actual rank in the Marines?

    a) Full Colonel   c) Major General
    b) Lieutenant Colonel   d) Captain

Photo courtesy the *Staten Island Register*

14. What type of columns are being used to support what remains of this temple in Segesta, Italy?

    a) Doric   c) Ionic
    b) Corinthian   d) Attic

Photo courtesy the *Staten Island Register*

15. At this writing the man on the left is the current White House chief-of-staff under President Reagan.

   a) Robert Dole   c) Frank Carlucci
   b) Alexander Haig   d) Howard Baker

Photo courtesy the *Staten Island Register*

16. The artist above gained a certain degree of fame by painting a can of Campbell's soup and predicting that everyone would be "famous for 15 minutes." What is the name of this artist *cum* philosopher?

   a) Marc Chagall   c) Andy Warhol
   b) Salvadore Dali   d) Norman Rockwell

Photo courtesy the *Staten Island Register*

17. In 1976 we celebrated the centennial of the Statue of Liberty. What is the full name of that monumental work of art?
    a) *The Modern Colossus* c) *Prometheus at Liberty*
    b) *Sic Semper Tyrannis* d) *Liberty Enlightening the World*

Photo courtesy 20th Century-Fox Film Corporation

18. Speaking of centennials, last year Sherlock Holmes—here played by Basil Rathbone—celebrated the hundredth anniversary of his first appearance in print. Which was the first Holmes novel published?

    a) *A Study in Scarlet* c) *The Sign of Four*
    b) *The Hound of the* d) *The Valley of Fear*
    Baskervilles

Photo courtesy the *Staten Island Register*

19. Above are the Pyramids at Giza, one of the Seven Wonders of the Ancient World. Approximately when were they constructed?

    a) c. 10,000 B.C.   c) c. 2,500 B.C.
    b) c. 5,000 B.C.   d) c. 1,000 B.C.

Photo courtesy the *Staten Island Register*

20. What was the name of the South Pacific island where atomic bomb tests were conducted in 1946?

    a) Bimini   c) Enola
    b) Bikini   d) Hispaniola

Photo courtesy the *Staten Island Register*

21. Pictured above is the woman whom history has dubbed "the first First Lady." Who is she?

a) Dolly Madison   c) Lucy Hayes
b) Martha Washington   d) Mary Todd Lincoln

Photo courtesy the *Staten Island Register*

22. In which state would you find the city of Cody, named after the famous frontiersman Buffalo Bill Cody?

a) Arizona   c) Oklahoma
b) Nevada   d) Wyoming

23. Which of the following artists should be credited with the painting above entitled *Female Nude?*

    a) Gauguin   c) Picasso
    b) Van Gogh   d) Dali

Photo courtesy the *Staten Island Register*

24. The woman above, a superb singer in her own right, was named the first female general director of the New York City Opera. Who is she?
    a) Beverly Sills   c) Roberta Peters
    b) Helen Traubel   d) Zinka Malanov

George Platt Lynes photo courtesy the *Staten Island Register*

25. Among this author's works are plays entitled *Summer and Smoke, The Rose Tattoo* and *Cat on a Hot Tin Roof*. Who is this famous playright?

   a) Eugene O'Neill   c) Tennessee Williams
   b) Thornton Wilder   d) Arthur Miller

Photo courtesy the *Staten Island Register*

26. What was the name given to the Rev. Jesse Jackson's supporters in his bid for the 1984 Democratic Presidential nomination?

   a) The Spectrum for   c) The Rainbow Coalition
       True Democracy
   b) Americans for Peace   d) Greenpeace
       and Progress

27. William Shakespeare is widely acclaimed as the world's greatest dramatist. What type of plays comprise the majority of the Bard's compositions?

    a) Comedies　　　　c) Romances
    b) History plays　　 d) Tragedies

28. What is the name of the eldest child of Prince Charles and Lady Diana? After all, the boy may someday become the King of England!

    a) Prince Andrew　　c) Prince Harold
    b) Prince Edward　　 d) Prince William

Photo courtesy the *Staten Island Register*

29. The man above has served as the conductor of both the New York and Israeli Philharmonic Orchestras. What is his name?

a) Aaron Copeland   c) Arthur Fiedler
b) Placido Domingo   d) Zuben Mehta

Photo courtesy the *Staten Island Register*

30. Lillian Hellman wrote a number of critically acclaimed plays, including *The Little Foxes* and *Watch on the Rhine*, but she is best remembered for which?

a) *The Matchmaker*   c) *Marty*
b) *The Children's Hour*   d) *Awake and Sing*

31. What is the name of the painting above?

    a) *Farm Life*

    b) *American Gothic*

    c) *A Study in Rural Life—The Artist's Parents*

    d) *Ma and Pa Kettle*

Photo courtesy the *Staten Island Register*

32. Walter Cronkite is generally regarded as the most influential newsman of the twentieth century. For which network did Cronkite work?

    a) Dumont

    b) ABC

    c) CBS

    d) NBC

Photo courtesy *Lou Giletta*

33. Pictured above is the longest suspension bridge in the world. Where is it located?

    a) San Francisco   c) Australia
    b) New York City   d) Great Britain

Photo courtesy the *Staten Island Register*

34. Leonard Bernstein composed the music for all except which of the following?

    a) *West Side Story*   c) *Requiem Mass*
    b) *"Trouble in Tahiti"*   d) *The Robber Bridegroom*

129

Photo courtesy the *Staten Island Register*

35. What is the title of author Stephen King's only *non-fiction* best seller?

   a) *The Dead Zone*   c) *Danse Macabre*
   b) *The Talisman*   d) *Eye of the Dragon*

Photo courtesy the *Staten Island Register*

36. The musician above has been dubbed "the King of Swing." His real name is

   a) Harry James   c) Benny Goodman
   b) Jimmy Dorsey   d) Glen Miller

Photo courtesy the *Staten Island Register*

37. Truman Capote is best remembered for his chilling tale *In Cold Blood*. In a lighter vein, he also wrote which of the following?

    a) *Sunday in Manhattan* c) *The Philadelphia Story*
    b) *Breakfast at Tiffany's* d) *Pal Joey*

38. The man above has been described as the individual most responsible for the shape and substance of the Constitution. Who is he?

    a) Alexander Hamilton   c) James Madison
    b) John Adams   d) Thomas Paine

39. This former Miss America served as New York City's Commissioner of Cultural Affairs until she resigned amid allegations of impropriety on her part. Who is she?

   a) Bess Meyerson   c) Phyllis George
   b) Lee Merriweather   d) Vanessa Williams

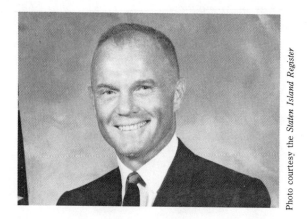

40. Colonel John Glenn was the first American to orbit the earth. He is now a United States senator. What state does the former astronaut represent?

   a) New Jersey   c) Idaho
   b) Iowa   d) Ohio

41. The man above was the very first senator from Texas. He also defeated the Mexican general Santa Anna and served as the first president of the Lone Star Republic. Who is he?

a) Colonel William Travis   c) Sam Houston
b) Stephen Austin   d) Frederick Dallas

42. The newsman above was a pioneer in both radio and television journalism. He covered the London blitz live and after the war helped to topple Sen. Joseph McCarthy. Who is he?

a) William Paley   c) Edward R. Murrow
b) Fred Friendly   d) Walter Winchell

Photo courtesy the *Staten Island Register*

43. Luciano Pavarotti is regarded as the world's foremost tenor. However, he recently appeared in his first film. What was it entitled?

a) *The Great Caruso*

b) *The Life of Mario Lanza*

c) *Yes, Giorgio*

d) *Hail, Mary*

Photo courtesy the *Staten Island Register*

44. During his terms as mayor of New York City, Edward I. Koch has done all except which of the following?

a) Write his autobiography

b) Work as a film critic

c) Appear on a Broadway stage

d) Reconcile with Donald Trump

Answers

1. c) Athena, which may help to explain why it is located in Athens

2. d) Gen. Douglas MacArthur

3. c) Pennsylvania

4. b) *The Syndics of the Cloth Hall*

5. d) *All My Sons*

6. c) Cornwallis

7. b) Alban W. Barkley. Incidentally, all of the other choices were 20th Century vice presidents.

8. b) Raisa

9. b) *La Gioconda*

10. b) Archibald Cox

11. c) *Gentlemen's Quarterly*

12. d) Ralph Nader

13. b) Lieutenant Colonel

14. a) Doric

15. d) Howard Baker

16. c) Andy Warhol

17. d) *Liberty Enlightening the World*

18. a) *A Study in Scarlet*

19. c) c. 2,500 B.C. Most experts date their actual construction around 2,700 B.C.

20. b) Bikini

21. c) Lucy Hayes

22. d) Wyoming

23. c) Picasso

24. a) Beverly Sills

25. c) Tennessee Williams

26. c) The Rainbow Coalition

27. a) Shakespeare wrote twelve comedies and only eleven tragedies.

136

28. d) Prince William

29. d) Zuben Mehta

30. b) *The Children's Hour*

31. b) *American Gothic,* by Grant Wood

32. c) CBS

33. b) New York City. The Verrazano Bridge links Staten Island and Brooklyn.

34. d) *The Robber Bridegroom*

35. c) *Danse Macabre*

36. c) Benny Goodman

37. b) *Breakfast at Tiffany's*

38. c) James Madison

39. a) Bess Meyerson

40. d) Ohio

41. c) Sam Houston

42. c) Edward R. Murrow

43. c) *Yes, Giorgio*

44. d) Reconcile with Donald Trump

Current Events and Recent History

1. On Monday, October 19, 1987, the New York Stock Exchange suffered through the single worst day in its history. Exactly, how many points did the market plummet?

   a) 228   c) 612
   b) 508   d) 1,057

2. This staggering loss represented approximately what percent of the entire market?

   a) 13 percent   c) 33 percent
   b) 23 percent   d) 51 percent

3. What was the name of the atheist who took her case to the United States Supreme Court and was thus responsible for ending prayer in public school?

   a) Gertrude Edderly   c) Madelyn Murry O'Hair
   b) Mary Baker Eddy   d) Bridgete Devlin

4. Now when E.F. Hutton talks, who will be listening most closely since this company merged with Hutton in late 1987?

   a) Kidder Peabody   c) Dean Witter
   b) Merrill Lynch   d) Shearson Lehman

5. What name did heiress Patty Hearst adopt when she became a member of the Symbionese Liberation Army?

   a) Cinque   c) Dove
   b) Tanya   d) Hafid

6. What was the name of the "inside trader" who had to pay the single largest fine in United States history: $50 million?

   a) Ivan Boesky   c) Charles Schwab
   b) Malcolm Forbes   d) L. Ron Hubbard

7. In what state is the Three Mile Island nuclear reactor located?

   a) Rhode Island   c) Pennsylvania
   b) New York   d) Ohio

8. How many times has Pope John Paul II visited the United States?

   a) 1   c) 3
   b) 2   d) 4

9. Oscar Arias Sanchez won the 1987 Nobel Peace Prize for his Central American peace plan. Of what nation is Sanchez president?

   a) Costa Rica   c) Nicaragua
   b) Guatamala   d) Honduras

10. In which year did Mao Zedong pass away, leaving control of China in the hands of Deng Xiaoping?

    a) 1976   c) 1978
    b) 1977   d) 1979

11. What was the name of the religious group founded by Jim Jones which ended in tragedy in Guyana?

    a) People's Commune   c) Church of the Savior
    b) Disciples of Christ   d) People's Temple

12. In which country is the Dalai Lama, spiritual leader of Tibetan Buddhism, living in exile?

    a) Bhutan   c) India
    b) Burma   d) Nepal

13. Which of these award-winning playwrights has yet to have his first play produced on Broadway?

    a) David Mamet   c) Herb Gardener
    b) Sam Shepard   d) Neil Simon

14. *Will* was the name of a book by which Watergate conspirator?

    a) Dean   c) Liddy
    b) Haldeman   d) Erhlichman

15. How many states did Walter Mondale carry in the 1984 Presidential election?

    a) None   c) 2
    b) 1   d) 3

16. What was the appropriately named yacht which figured prominently in the Gary Hart-Donna Rice affair?

    a) *Good Times*   c) *California Dreamin'*
    b) *Monkey Business*   d) *No Excuses*

17. What did Dennis Connor do in 1987 for which he deserves to be remembered?

    a) Landed his plane in   c) Was rejected as a nominee
        Red Square   to the Supreme Court
    b) Was freed by his   d) Won the America's Cup
        Iranian captors

18. In the wake of the Iran-Contra affair, Howard Baker was named White House Chief of Staff. Whom did he replace?

    a) Edward Meese   c) James Baker
    b) Donald Regan   d) Raymond Donovan

19. Which major U.S. oil company filed for bankruptcy as the result of a suit brought against it by Pennzoil?

    a) Exxon   c) Shell
    b) Gulf   d) Texaco

20. Soviet premier Mikhil Gorbachev has announced that the Soviet Union will pursue a policy of *glasnost*. How does that term translate into English?

    a) Truthfulness   c) Openness
    b) Peacefulness   d) Capitalism

21. With what timely subject did *The Tower Report* concern itself?

    a) AIDS   c) The Kennedy assassination
    b) The Iran-Contra
       Affair   d) The Watergate hearings

22. What was the first movie on video cassette to carry a commercial advertisement?

    a) *Crocodile Dundee*   c) *Top Gun*
    b) *Fatal Attraction*   d) *Raiders of the Lost Ark*

23. How much was the USFL awarded in its lawsuit against the NFL?

    a) $.01   c) $1.00
    b) $.10   d) $100.00

24. In which year did Anwar Sadat and Menahem Begin sign the peace treaty which President Carter had helped to negotiate?

    a) 1977   c) 1979
    b) 1978   d) 1980

25. We stated earlier that in 1987 a painting entitled *Irises* sold for a record $53.9 million. Who painted those costly *fleurs*?

    a) Matisse   c) Van Gogh
    b) Monet   d) Picasso

26. What was the amount television evangelist Oral Roberts claimed he had to raise or face the ''fact'' that God would ''call him home''?

    a) $3 million   c) $6 million
    b) $4 million   d) $8 million

27. As of 1987, how many countries had conducted nuclear bomb tests?

    a) 4   c) 6
    b) 5   d) 7

28. The world's newest nation obtained its independence in 1984. Which of the following countries can lay claim to that distinction?

    a) Brunei   c) Tuvalu
    b) Suriname   d) Vanuatu

29. The world's longest railroad tunnel—a stretch of some 33.5 miles—was completed in 1985. This tunnel is twenty miles longer than the previous record-holder. In what country or countries was it built?

    a) England and France   c) Japan
    b) Soviet Union   d) U.S.A.

30. The biggest corporate merger to date—outside of the oil industry—occurred in 1985, when General Electric bought which of the following companies for $6.28 billion?

    a) Renault Motors   c) Dow Chemical
    b) RCA Corporation d) Texas Instruments

31. It what year was AT&T ordered to split up? Hint: it was the same year the ERA was defeated.

    a) 1982   c) 1984
    b) 1983   d) 1985

32. The Gramm-Rudman bill was a last-ditch effort to end the huge federal deficit. In which year did President Reagan sign it into law?

    a) 1984   c) 1986
    b) 1985   d) 1987

33. Which Caribbean country was Jean-Claude Duvalier—"president for life"—forced to flee in February of 1986?

    a) Dominican Republic   c) El Salvador
    b) Haiti   d) Costa Rica

34. Who headed up the committee to celebrate the bicentennial of the Constitution?

    a) Earl Warren   c) Lee Iacocca
    b) Warren Burger   d) Ronald Reagan

35. On February 26, 1986, the United States chose its first official poet laureate. Who was the honoree?

    a) Rod McKuen   c) Stanley Kunitz
    b) Robert Penn Warren   d) Robert Frost
                               (posthumously)

36. Where was the first Reagan-Gorbachev summit meeting held?

    a) Geneva, Switzerland c) Washington, D.C.
    b) Reykjavik, Iceland   d) Moscoe, Russia

37. Which flying giant recently acquired People's Express as well as a squadron of smaller airlines?

    a) Eastern   c) Northwest Orient
    b) Texas Air   d) Pan Am

38. To which South American country were U.S. soldiers dispatched in an attempt to locate and destroy secret cocaine-processing laboratories?

    a) Argentina   c) Colombia
    b) Bolivia   d) Venezuela

39. In 1987 the United States finally chose an official "national floral emblem." What is our national flower?

    a) Carnation   c) Apple blossom
    b) Daisy   d) Rose

40. In which section of the Soviet Union is the Chernobyl nuclear plant located?
    a) Georgia   c) Siberia
    b) Ukraine   d) Moldavia

41. What is the proper name for the defense plan which President Reagan has termed "Star Wars"?

    a) Strategic Defense   c) Outer Space Defense
       Initiative   System
    b) American Protection   d) Reagan's Folly
       Program

42. For which publication was journalist Nicholas Daniloff working when he was seized by the Soviets as a spy?

    a) *Time*   c) *U.S. News and World
                                  Report*
    b) *Newsweek*   d) *America*

43. Actress Shirley MacLaine detailed her out-of-body experiences and meetings with extra-terrestrials in which book?

    a) *Many Mansions*

    b) *Out on a Limb*

    c) *Another Decade — Another Life*

    d) *E.T.—Phoning Home*

44. How many states did Jimmy Carter, the incumbent President, carry when he lost his bid for reelection in 1980?

    a) 2

    b) 4

    c) 6

    d) 8

45. To date, how many different space shuttles have voyaged into outer space?

    a) 3

    b) 4

    c) 5

    d) 6

46. In which year were hurricanes first named after males as well as females?

    a) 1976

    b) 1977

    c) 1978

    d) 1979

47. Who was the first person to receive an artificial heart?

    a) Dr. Barney Clark

    b) William Schroeder

    c) William DeVries

    d) The Tin Man In *The Wizard of Oz*

48. Who is the head of the Polish trade union known as Solidarity?

    a) Lech Walesa

    b) Wojciech Jaruzelski

    c) Jozef Glemp

    d) Zdzislaw Ruravz

49. In May 1982 the Rev. Sun Myung Moon was convicted of tax fraud. Of what church was Moon the head?

    a) People's Temple

    b) Unification Church

    c) Ecumenical Cathedral

    d) Hari Krishnas

50. Earlier we asked about the subject of the Tower Commission's report. Now we'd like to know how many men comprised the Tower Commission?

    a) 3   c) 7
    b) 5   d) 8

51. In 1985 Raymond Donovan earned a degree of notoriety when he became the first sitting member of a President's Cabinet ever to be indicted. What position had he held?

    a) Secretary of the   c) Secretary of State
       Interior
    b) Secretary of Labor   d) Attorney General

52. Jan Kemp won a $2.5 million judgment against a major university which had fired her when she criticized the institution for giving passing grades to failing football players. Which university had employed Kemp?

    a) University of Texas   c) University of Georgia
    b) University of   d) Southern Methodist
       Tennessee   University

53. A 1985-86 best-selling novel by Alice Walker later became a motion picture. Which was the title?

    a) *Terms of Endearment* c) *The Color Purple*
    b) *Educating Rita*   d) *An Officer and a Gentleman*

54. What is the first name of Judge Ginsburg, President Reagan's second choice for the vacant seat on the Supreme Court?

    a) Michael   c) Douglas
    b) Robert   d) Alan

55. Democratic senator Joseph Biden withdrew from the Presidential race in 1987 amid charges that he had plagiarized his speeches. What state does Biden represent?

a) Florida   c) Minnesota
b) Maine   d) Delaware

56. What was the name of the young woman whose allegations against Jim Bakker caused an unholy row in the PTL?

a) Fahn Hall   c) Tammy Bakker
b) Jessica Hahn   d) Fanny Fox

Answers

1. b) 508

2. b) 23 percent

3. c) Madelyn Murry O'Hair

4. d) Shearson Lehman

5. b) Tanya

6. a) Ivan Boesky

7. c) Pennsylvania

8. b) 2

9. a) Costa Rica

10. a) 1976

11. d) People's Temple

12. c) India

13. b) Sam Shepard

14. c) G. Gordon Liddy

15. a) 1 — Minnesota. Mondale also carried the District of Columbia.

16. b) *Monkey Business*

17. d) Won the America's Cup

18. b) Donald Regan

19. d) Texaco

20. c) Openness

21. b) The Iran-Contra affair

22. c) *Top Gun* (an ad for Diet Pepsi)

23. c) $1.00

24. c) 1979

25. c) Van Gogh

26. d) $8 million

27. b) 5: The U.S., the U.S.S.R., Great Britain, France and China.

28. a) Brunei

29. c) Japan

30. b) RCA Corporation

31. a) 1982

32. b) 1985

33. b) Haiti

34. b) Warren Burger

35. b) Robert Penn Warren

36. b) Reykjavik, Iceland

37. b) Texas Air

38. b) Bolivia

39. d) Rose

40. b) Ukraine

41. a) Strategic Defense Initiative

42. c) *U.S. News and World Report*

43. b) *Out on a Limb*

44. c) 6

45. b) 4

46. d) 1979

47. a) Dr. Barney Clark

48. a) Lech Walesa

49. b) Unification Church

50. a) 3

51. b) Secretary of Labor

52. c) University of Georgia

53. c) *The Color Purple*

54. c) Douglas

55. d) Delaware

56. b) Jessica Hahn

Final Examination

Up until now, all the questions have been multiple choice—or at least multiple guess. This chapter requires a broad range of exact knowledge in a variety of diverse fields. All the questions are short-answer types, and you either know the answer or you do not; however, guessing is still permitted.

1. What is the most common surname in the world?

2. Who created daylight savings time?

3. Who is the only president of the United States ever to have served as Chief Justice of the Supreme Court?

4. What is the name of the world's largest diamond, which weighs in at 970 carats?

5. How many different political parties have had their candidates elected President of the United States, and how many can you name?

6. Although commonly referred to as "Capitol Hill," the Capitol Building actually sits atop a hill with an altogether different name. What is the real name of Capitol Hill?

7. As long as we're on the subject of hills, Rome was built on seven of them. How many of those fabled hills can you name?

8. One more hill question: What was the name of the hill where the Battle of Bunker Hill took place?

9. While a number of words in English can lay claim to the fact that they contain all five vowels, only two contain the vowels in their proper alphabetical order. Can you name either one?

10. How many times did King Henry VIII marry, and how many of his wives can you name?

11. What is the word *laser* an acronym for?

12. The marathon originated in Greece after the Athenians had defeated the Persians at the Battle of Marathon. Exactly how long is a true marathon, and what was the name of that first long-distance runner?

13. The term "liberal arts" was coined in the Middle Ages. Originally, how many liberal arts were there, and how many can you name?

14. At present, how many positions are there in the President's Cabinet?

15. What is the name of the world's largest glacier? It is located in Antarctica and measures 250 miles in length.

16. "It was the best of times; it was the worst of times" were the opening lines of Charles Dickens's *A Tale of Two Cities*. What were the two cities alluded to in the title?

17. By what name is the Earl of Locksley more commonly known?

18. In the Spanish-Amercan War, the battle cry was "Remember the *Maine!*" Where was the *Maine* when she was sunk?

19. The gerund always funtions as what part of speech?

20. What element is represented by the chemical symbol *Fe* in the periodic table?

21. Mikhail Gorbachev was recently honored as *Time Magazines's* Man of the Year for 1987. Who was the first individual so honored by that magazine?

22. On the average, who have higher I.Q.'s, men or women?

23. In which great science-fiction novel is time reckoned in years A.F.—After Ford?

24. Alphabetically speaking, what are the first and last countries in the world?

25. Who was the first man to translate the Bible into that vulgar tongue, Latin?

26. What was the name of the first U.S. space shuttle, launched in 1981?

27. What university can lay claim to being the first established in America?

28. Who is credited with composing *The Brandenburg Concertos*?

29. As long as we're discussing music, what is the name of the man who composed the opera *Carmen*?

30. Sticking with the fine arts, which French painter developed the artistic technique known as pointillism?

31. The Home Insurance Building in Chicago lays claim to what distinction?

32. *Reader's Digest* is the magazine with the world's largest circulation. Which periodical has the next greatest number of readers?

33. In what year was the first test-tube baby born?

34. Can you name either or both of the litigants involved in the 1973 Supreme Court case which legalized abortion?

35. In that same vein, what was the first country to leagalize abortion? It happened in 1935.

36. Who was the first man to reach the South Pole? He was also the first man to sail the Northeast Passage by the North Pole.

37. As of 1987, what was the approximate population of the world, give or take a million or two?

38. After Lenin's death, who fought with Stalin for control of the Communist Party? He was later assissinated in Mexico, presumably on Stalin's orders.

39. As long as we're talking about Russian history, who was crowned the first czar of Russia?

40. The Punic Wars were fought between what two cities?

41. Who was the only American admiral who was also an admiral in the Russian navy?

42. What did the 26th Amendment to the Constitution, which was passed in 1971, do?

43. Although it has not yet happened the question has arisen: Legally, can a convicted criminal be elected President of the United States?

44. Whom did Mikhail Gorbachev succeed as the head of the Communist Party in the U.S.S.R., and in what year did he become the Soviet premier?

45. In which European city is the International Court of Justice to be found?

46. What is the youngest state east of the Mississippi?

47. On what language is 72 percent of the English language based?

48. America has the C.I.A. and Russia has the K.G.B. What is the name of Israel's world-renowned intelligence agency?

49. What is the largest lake in the world? Hint: It's not called a lake.

50. Speaking of large, on what continent would you find the world's largest rain forest?

51. What is the average pulse rate of a healthy adult?

52. What was the name of the Swiss psychologist who broke with Freudianism and coined the term ''collective unconsciousness''?

53. Can you name the theologian who claimed that the world had been created at exactly 10 a.m. on Sunday, October 26, in the year 4004 B.C.?

54. What was the name of the first vessel in the United States navy?

55. We've come a long way since then, but you ought to be able to recall the name of the first atomic-powered submarine. What was it?

56. What is the value of π carried to five places?

57. What is the metrical prefix for one billion?

58. What are the tallest plants in the world?

59. What author wrote the oft-quoted line, "A rose is a rose is a rose is a rose"?

60. Diamonds may be a girl's best friend, but they are not the rarest gemstone. What is?

61. Within 3 percent, how much of the earth's surface is dry land?

62. What was the name of the young girl with whom the poet Dante fell in love? She also served as his guide through *Il Paradiso* in the *Divine Comedy*?

63. What does the musical term *allegro* mean?

64. What is the more *familiar* name by which we know Anna Mary Robertson?

65. What European city would you visit to see the famous Notre Dame Cathedral?

66. How many months do not take their names from either people or gods?

67. *Sputnik* was the name of the first Russian satellite. What was the name of the first American satellite, which was launched in 1958?

68. In that same vein, what was the name of the first space station launched by the United States, in 1973?

69. Which state has the highest annual normal precipitation rate, with more than 64 inches of rainfall annually? At the other end of the spectrum, the state with the lowest precipitation rate receives an average of only 7 inches of rain a year. Can you name that one as well?

70. Halley's comet last appeared in 1985-86. When will it next return so that people on earth can see it?

71. What is the fastest moving animal in the world?

72. Genetically speaking, which is the dominant trait: large eyes or small eyes?

73. What is the longest river in Europe?

74. Who was the first U.S. president actually to be born in the country of the United States?

75. Where did Lee surrender to Grant to end the Civil War?

76. With what invention is Alessandro Volta charged?

77. Who succeeded Kurt Waldheim as Secretary General of the United Nations?

78. In which country did the Industrial Revolution have its beginnings?

159

79. Within two years, how long did Prohibition—which Herbert Hoover called a "noble experiment"—last?

80. Can you name the only country in the world that begins with the letter *O*?

81. What are Romeo and Juliet's last names?

82. Whom did Napoleon marry after he and Josephine were divorced in 1809?

83. From divorce to marriage: Who was the only president to be married in the White House?

84. What is the mission of San Antonio de Valero more commonly known as?

85. How many colleges make up the prestigious Ivy League?

86. The term *saphairistike* was originally used as the name of what popular sport?

87. Perhaps counterculture started with the advent of rock'n'roll. Who is generally credited with coining that term?

88. What is the primary interest of an ichthyologist?

89. According to the Islamic religion, what date is the start of the lunar new year?

90. In a normal year of 365 days, what is the date of the exact middle of the year?

91. In which crusade did King Richard I of England participate?

92. 1988 is a very special year for Australia. What special event will that country be commemorating this year?

93. In which year did the French Revolution begin?

94. Alan Shepard was the first American in space, but he was not the first man in space. What was the name of that first Russian cosmonaut, who beat Shepard into space by a mere 23 days?

95. In that same vein, Sally Ride was the first American woman in space, but the first Russian woman was launched in 1963. Can you recall her name?

96. Kinhasa is the capital city of which African nation?

97. What was the name of the American who invented the cotton gin?

98. Which United States president is credited with inventing the folding bed and the swivel chair?

99. Who was the first Christian religious leader to stress the idea of predestination?

100. Who were the opposing attorneys in the famous Scopes Monkey Trial?

Answers

1. Chang is the most common last name, while Muhammed is the most common first name.

2. Benjamin Franklin

3. William H. Taft

4. The Excelsior

5. Five political parties have had their candidates elected President: the Federalists, the Democratic-Republicans, the Whigs, the Democrats and the Republicans.

6. The Capitol Building actually sits atop Jenkins Hill.

7. The "seven hills of Rome" are the Aventine, the Caelian, the Capitoline, the Exquiline, the Palatine, the Quirinal and the Viminal.

8. The Battle of Bunker Hill was actually fought on Breed's Hill in Charlestown, Massachusetts.

9. The only two words that contain all five vowels in alphabetical order are *facetious* and *abstemious*.

10. Henry wed six times. His wives were Catherine of Aragon, Anne Boleyn, Lady Jane Seymour, Anne of Cleves, Catherine Howard, and Catherine Parr.

11. Light Amplification by Stimulated Emmission of Radiation

12. A true marathon is 26 miles 385 yards, and the first marathoner was a messenger named Pheidippides, who actually only ran about 22 miles, uttered the Greek word *Nike*, which means victory, and dropped dead—probably of heat exhaustion.

13. Originally, there were seven liberal arts: the *trivium* consisted of grammar, logic and rhetoric; and the *quadrivium* consisted of arithmetic, geometry, astronomy and music.

14. There are currently fourteen positions in the President's Cabinet.

15. Lambert Glacier

16 The title refers to London and Paris.

17. Robin Hood

18. The *Maine* was moored in the harbor at Havana, Cuba.

19. A gerund is a word that ends in *ing* and functions as a noun.

20. *Fe* is the chemical symbol for iron.

21. Charles Lindbergh

22. Women

23. In Aldous Huxley's *Brave New World*

24. Afghanistan and Zimbabwe

25. St. Jerome

26. The *Columbia*

27. Harvard

28. Bach

29. Georges Bizet

30. Georges Seurat

31. It is considered the first skyscraper.

32. *TV Guide* is number two and trying harder.

33. 1978

34. The case that legalized abortion was *Roe* vs. *Wade*.

35. Iceland

36. Roald Amundsen

37. 4.9 billion

38. Leon Trotsky

39. Ivan IV

40. Rome and Carthage

41. John Paul Jones

42. It lowered the voting age to 18.

43. According to the Constitution, there is nothing prohibiting a convicted criminal from being elected President.

44. Gorbachev succeeded Konstantin Chernenko in 1985.

45. The Hague, in the Netherlands

46. West Virginia

47. Latin

48. The Mossad

49. The Caspian Sea

50. South America

51. 72 beats per minute

52. Karl Jung

53. James Ussher, Archbishop of Armagh

54. The *Hannah*

55. *Nautilus*

56. 3.14159

57. Giga

58. The giant redwoods of California

59. Gertrude Stein

60. The ruby

61. 29 percent

62. Beatrice

63. *Allegro* literally means ''merry,'' but musically it means lively or fast.

64. Grandma Moses

65. Paris, France

66. 5: April, September, October, November and December.

67. *Explorer I*

68. *Skylab*

69. Alabama has the highest, and Arizona has the lowest.

70. Halley's comet appears every 76.1 years; it is scheduled to return in the years 2061-62.

71. The peregrine falcon has been clocked at 217 miles per hour in a dive.

72. Large eyes are dominant.

73. The Danube

74. Martin Van Buren

75. Appamattox

76. The first electrical battery

77. Javier Perez de Cuellar of Peru

78. England

79. Prohibition lasted a little less than fifteen years.

80. Oman

81. Montague and Capulet, respectively

82. Princess Marie Louise of Austria

83. Grover Cleveland

84. The Alamo

85. 8: Brown, Columbia, Cornell, Dartmouth, Harvard, Pennsylvania, Princeton and Yale

86. Tennis

87. Alan Freed

88. Fish

89. July 16

90. July 2

91. The Third Crusade

92. Its bicentennial

93. 1789

94. Yuri Gagarin

95. Valentina V. Tereshkova

96. Zaire

97. Eli Whitney

98. Thomas Jefferson

99. John Calvin

100. William Jennings Bryan and Clarence Darrow